C000084724

Impact English

MIKE GOULD (SERIES EDITOR), KIM RICHARDSON, MARY GREEN & JOHN MANNION

Key Stage 3 – Year 9 • Student Book 1

Contents

① Count Sylvius calls

Aims

▶ Read an extract from a short story

▶ Review and develop your writing of more complex sentences (S1)

▶ Explore how a text reflects the time in which it was written and what makes it popular today (R15)

▶ Write about a villainous character

This text is from a short story by Sir Arthur Conan Doyle about the famous detective, Sherlock Holmes.

It was, therefore, an empty room into which Billy, a minute later, ushered Count Sylvius. The famous game-shot, sportsman and man-about-town was a big, swarthy fellow, with a formidable dark moustache, shading a cruel, thin-lipped mouth, and surmounted by a long, curved nose, like the beak of an eagle. He was well dressed, but his brilliant necktie, shining
5   pin and glittering rings were flamboyant in their effect. As the door closed behind him he looked round him with fierce, startled eyes, like one who suspects a trap at every turn. Then he gave a violent start as he saw the impassive head and the collar of the dressing-gown which projected above the armchair in the window. At first his expression was one of pure amazement. Then the light of a horrible hope gleamed in his dark, murderous eyes. He took
10   one more glance round to see that there were no witnesses, and then, on tiptoe, his thick stick half raised, he approached the silent figure. He was crouching for his final spring and blow when a cool, sardonic voice greeted him from the open bedroom door.
        'Don't break it, Count! Don't break it!'
        The assassin staggered back, amazement in his convulsed face. For an instant he half raised
15   his loaded cane once more, as if he would turn his violence from the effigy to the original; but there was something in that steady grey eye and mocking smile which caused his hand to sink to his side.
        'It's a pretty little thing,' said Holmes, advancing towards the image. 'Tavernier, the French modeller, made it. He is as good at waxworks as your friend Straubenzee is at air-guns.'
20   'Air-guns, sir! What do you mean?'
        'Put your hat and stick on the side-table. Thank you! Pray take a seat. Would you care to

put your revolver out also? Oh, very good, if you prefer to sit upon it. Your visit is really most opportune, for I wanted badly to have a few minutes' chat with you.'

The Count scowled, with heavy, threatening eyebrows. 'I too, wished to have some words with you, Holmes. That is why I am here. I won't deny that I intended to assault you just now.'

25

Holmes swung his leg on the edge of the table. 'I rather gathered that you had some idea of the sort in your head,' said he. 'But why these personal attentions?'

'Because you have gone out of your way to annoy me. Because you have put your creatures upon my track.'

30

'My creatures! I assure you no!'

'Nonsense! I have had them followed. Two can play at that game, Holmes.'

'It is a small point, Count Sylvius, but perhaps you would kindly give me my prefix when you address me. You can understand that, with my routine of work, I should find myself on familiar terms with half the rogues' gallery, and you will agree that exceptions are invidious.'

35

'Well, Mr Holmes, then.'

'Excellent! But I assure you you are mistaken about my alleged agents.'

Count Sylvius laughed contemptuously. 'Other people can observe as well as you. Yesterday there was an old sporting man. Today it was an elderly woman. They held me in view all day.'

40

'Really, sir, you compliment me. Old Baron Dowson said the night before he was hanged that in my case what the law had gained the stage had lost. And now you give my little impersonations your kindly praise!'

'It was you – you yourself?'

Holmes shrugged his shoulders. 'You can see in the corner the parasol which you so politely handed to me in the Minories before you began to suspect.'

45

'If I had known, you might never—'

'Have seen this humble home again. I was well aware of it. We all have neglected opportunities to deplore. As it happens, you did not know, so here we are!'

The Count's knotted brows gathered more heavily over his menacing eyes. 'What you say only makes the matter worse. It was not your agents, but your play-acting, busy-body self! You admit that you have dogged me. Why?'

50

'Come now, Count. You used to shoot lions in Algeria.'

'Well?'

'But why?'

55

'Why? The sport – the excitement – the danger!'

'And no doubt, to free the country from a pest?'

'Exactly!'

'My reasons in a nutshell!'

The Count sprang to his feet, and his hand involuntarily moved back to his hip-pocket.

60

'Sit down, sir, sit down! There was another, more practical reason. I want that yellow diamond!'

Count Sylvius lay back in his chair with an evil smile.

'Upon my word!' said he.

swarthy dark-skinned	**opportune** convenient
flamboyant brightly-coloured or decorated	**invidious** creating resentment
impassive showing no emotion	**contemptuously** in a scornful way
sardonic mocking	**deplore** object strongly
	involuntarily without meaning to

Key Reading

Narrative texts

This text is a **narrative** or story. Its main **purpose** is to entertain us.

The key main features of this text are:

● It has a structure that includes an **introduction** and the **development** of the plot (the complication, the climax and resolution all come later). For example, we are introduced to a new character, Count Sylvius. We then find out why Holmes wants to see Count Sylvius and what could develop from this.

● It uses **expressive and descriptive language**. For example, 'The Count *scowled*, with *heavy*, threatening *eyebrows*.'

● It has **characters**, who the story is about. There is also a **narrator**, who tells the story in either the first person (I/we) or the third person (he/she/it), for example, 'Holmes swung *his* leg on the edge of the table.'

● It uses **dialogue/direct speech** to develop the story, or tell us about characters, for example, "Sit down, sir, sit down! There was another, more practical reason. I want that yellow diamond!"

1 **a)** We are introduced to Count Sylvius at the start of the extract. Note down **one detail** about his face from paragraph 1. Try to choose a description that is striking and creates a strong picture in your mind.

b) Note down **two words or phrases** that tell you that Count Sylvius is a villain, not a hero.

2 What are the **first spoken words** in this extract? Who is speaking? (Take care in your answer, as the speaker is not obvious.)

3 Count Sylvius thinks that Holmes has paid people to follow him. What has **actually happened**?

● ●

Purpose

4 Conan Doyle **entertains the reader** in a number of ways. Look at the suggestions below. In pairs, discuss which of these are correct. You will need to check the story carefully.

● The writer creates strong characters that are easy to picture in our minds.

● The writer makes us laugh as we read.

● The writer tricks us into thinking something will happen, but it doesn't.

Reading for meaning

The Sherlock Holmes stories were written at the end of the 19th century and the start of the 20th century – about a hundred years ago.

R15

5 If we look at the stories closely, we can see that they reflect the time in which they were written. Look through the text and see if you can find evidence for the following. **Copy the table** and fill in the final column.

Focus	What you are looking for	Reference (line number and words)
Language change (a word or phrase we wouldn't use much now)	A word meaning 'please' as in 'please sit down'	
Changes in the way we live (something that doesn't happen much now)	Hunting endangered species in a foreign country	

Focus on: Complex sentences and added detail

One example of a **simple sentence** from the text is as follows:

SUBJECT (the person doing the action)

Holmes shrugged his shoulders.

VERB (what is being done)

OBJECT (the thing that receives the action)

There are not many simple sentences like this in the text. If the sentence had been written as follows, it would be a **complex sentence**:

> Holmes shrugged his shoulders, so that the Count could see he wasn't scared.

The **conjunction** links the first part to the second. This second section (or clause) would not make sense on its own.

S1

6 Here are two more simple sentences from the text. Turn them into **complex sentences** by adding further information after the conjunction.

   a) Count Sylvius lay back in his chair with an evil smile, *although* he…

   b) Count Sylvius laughed contemptuously, *after* Holmes had…

7 The key point is that good writers **add further detail** and information to create a picture in the reader's mind. In this next complex sentence, the main clause is in italics. The writer has added two extra bits of information in clauses on either side of it:

> As the door closed behind him *he looked round him with fierce, startled eyes*, like one who suspects a trap at every turn.

   a) Which clause tells us **when** this happens?

   b) Which clause compares Count Sylvius to a **hunted animal**?

9

Key Writing

8 This story is all about two powerful characters – Sherlock Holmes and Count Sylvius. You are going to **write the opening to a story**. It will introduce a villain like Count Sylvius.

a) First, make notes on your villain's **appearance**. Describe **three features** of their face using at least one adjective. For example:

'She had a *short, ugly nose*.'

'Her hair was .... and ....'

'She had a .... mouth.'

b) The story will start with your villain entering the room, so make notes on their **thoughts and actions** as they come in, for example, 'laughing madly'.

c) Then **write the opening paragraph** to your story. Try to describe how your villain moves and what their thoughts are, as well as how they look. If you can, include one complex sentence using a conjunction such as 'although', 'because' or 'that'.

You could use this example to get you started:

Name of your villain

The door opened and .... entered. He/she had...

② The Tolkien disease

Aims

▶ Read part of a biography about a famous author

▶ Explore how a writer makes a point in an unusual way (W7)

▶ Look at different ways of beginning narratives (Wr5)

▶ Write about someone using a metaphor

The following text is from the opening of a biography by Susan Ang about the author J. R. R. Tolkien called *The Master of the Rings*. But, has he done something terrible?

J. R. R. Tolkien, author of *The Hobbit* and *The Lord of the Rings*, is perhaps the greatest fantasy writer ever to have lived; he is certainly the most influential. But there is a darker side to this great man. He is also the creator of one of the most dangerous and communicable
5 diseases known to man: Tolkienomania. This disease can be described as follows:

Most often transmitted through reading, although it can also be communicated through other media, such as film. Symptoms: during the initial stages of the disease, patient may suffer loss of appetite and refuse to
10 *appear for meals. Eyes will be glazed. Sufferers may turn violent or experience serious anxiety attacks should the next volume not be to hand. In the later stages of the disease, the glazed look disappears, but only to be replaced by a fanatic gleam in the eye. This and the bulging pocket or rucksack – in which will be stored a copy/multiple copies of* The Lord of
15 the Rings *with which to infect others – are warnings that the disease is about to be transmitted. No known cure exists.*

Behind this light-heartedness lies a serious point. The chief characteristic of fans of *The Lord of the Rings* (the book) is a single-mindedness about the worth and wonder of the work itself. Even
20 before the Peter Jackson film cast its spell over cinema audiences around the world ('One film to bring them all and in the darkness bind them', as Gandalf might have said), the world has been full of Tolkienomanes. In the UK in 1996, the bookshop chain Waterstones ran a poll for the Top 100 books of the century. *The Lord of the Rings*
25 topped the poll, beating the likes of George Orwell's *Nineteen Eighty-*

four and J. D. Salinger's *The Catcher in the Rye* (*The Hobbit* came nineteenth). The book itself has never been out of print since its first publication in 1954–5, and has sold over 100 million copies. And for years the world has been full of Tolkien societies, Tolkien criticism,
30 Tolkien webpages and women calling themselves 'Galadriel'.

The film of *The Lord of the Rings* is a very good film. It is all in glorious technicolour, gives a visual concreteness to Middle-earth, which is at one level very satisfying, and has some breathtaking moments (the Moria sequences are, in particular, quite superb). It is
35 all very enjoyable. But the film is not the book.

What is it that makes the book so great? As Tolkien himself said, *The Lord of the Rings* is primarily an 'exciting story'. That was what he thought the people who had enjoyed it had responded to and this, he said, was how it had been written. But it is not only an
40 exciting story, or rather, it is not just because it is an exciting story that people have been reading it for nearly fifty years. So, what is it about Tolkien's work, in particular *The Lord of the Rings*, which has prompted and continues to prompt such responses? Why does it enthral, excite and, perhaps above all, move readers? What makes it
45 work? There are probably no short answers to these questions. But the fact that his work is read today as avidly, if not more avidly, than it was when it was first published, and has a breadth of appeal clearly shown by its translation into more than thirty-five languages, suggests that *The Lord of the Rings* deals in universals. It would not
50 otherwise have transcended time and culture as it has.

Key Reading

Analysis texts

This text is an **analysis**. Its **purpose** is to look at something that has happened and explore and seek to understand it.

The main features of this text are:

- It separates information and evidence into **clear paragraphs**. For example, the first paragraph explains who Tolkien is.

- It asks and addresses **key questions**, for example, 'What is it that makes the book so great?'

- It refers to **quotes** and **sources** to back up these questions, for example, 'As Tolkien himself said, *The Lord of the Rings* is primarily an "exciting story"'.

- It **weighs up evidence** using **connectives** that draw out contrasts. For example, the writer compares the film and the original book: '*But* the film is not the book.'

1 The text is divided into several paragraphs. What is the **second paragraph** (in italics) about?

2 The writer asks lots of **questions** in the text. How many can you find?

3 In order to show how good the book is, the author refers to some evidence – a '**poll**' from 1996. Who conducted the poll, and what did it show?

Purpose

4 What is really interesting about this text is that the writer gains our attention in an unusual way. She describes 'Tolkienomania' as a disease.

    a) Why is this an **unusual** way to describe how fans of the book behave?

    b) In pairs, discuss what the main **symptoms** of this disease are.

Reading for meaning

The writer could have just said that the book was very popular and that people couldn't stop themselves reading it. Instead she uses a **metaphor**. This is when a writer writes about something as if it is something else. In this case: *Loving the book = an addiction, or disease.*

The writer also **exaggerates** to make her point. For example, '…sufferers (fans of the book) may turn violent…should the next volume not be to hand.'

W7

5 Discuss these questions in pairs:

    a) Does the writer really think that being a fan is **dangerous**?

    b) Is this a **real disease**?

6 Here is a metaphor that works in a similar way: 'Your life is a mountain climb.'

Write down **one way** in which life is like a mountain climb.

Focus on: Different ways of opening texts

The author chose to open her book about J. R. R. Tolkien by comparing the popularity of *The Lord of the Rings* to a disease. She even wrote it like a medical warning.

However, there are other ways of making the beginnings of texts interesting. Susan Ang could have started by asking questions straight away; this is clever because the reader begins to want to know the answers. For example:

> J. R. R. Tolkien is one of the greatest writers who ever lived. But why are his books so loved? And where did he get his ideas from? What do we really know about this man, and his life?

This technique also leads the reader to believe that the text will answer these questions if they read on. It is common in analysis texts to set out the different aspects of the topic to be analysed at the start of the text.

Often the first question begins with the connective 'but' to show that ideas that contrast with or challenge the original statement will follow. For example, 'But why are his books so loved?'

Wr5 **7** Come up with a set of **three or four questions** to add to an opening statement about a favourite team or a pop star.

Here is an example of how one question might look:

'................. are the greatest team ever. But why...?'

Or this:

'................. is the greatest pop star/band ever. But why...?'

Use a range of question starters to add variety, for example:

● 'Why?' ● 'How?' ● 'Where?' ● 'When?' ● 'What?'.

Key Writing

8 Now try to **imitate the author's idea about a disease** in a description of your favourite football team or pop star. For example:

> 'Gunnermania' is a dreadful disease. It is at its worst on Saturdays when Arsenal play at home. The sufferer leaps out of bed and cannot stop him or herself putting on red and white clothes...

If you are an Arsenal fan, continue the idea above. If you are a fan of another team, start a new one.

If you are writing about a pop star you could begin...

> .....[name of star + 'ania']... is an awful disease. The disease is caught when the sufferer is close to a television and sees their star perform. The first symptom is to grab the remote control when the programme ends and feverishly flick through channels to search for a new fix.

Teenage con man

Aims

▶ Read a review of a film based on a real criminal's life

▶ Explore how a non-fiction text can convey information in an interesting way (Wr7)

▶ Analyse the use of rhetorical devices (R12)

▶ Write about a scene from a film or television programme

The following text is a review of the film *Catch Me If You Can*.

Catch Me If You Can

Leonardo DiCaprio effortlessly charms his way through Steven Spielberg's zippy, lightweight chase thriller, the real-life tale of con man extraordinaire Frank Abagnale Jr.

It's fortunate that **Catch Me If You Can** is based on a true story, for
5 otherwise film-goers, on exiting cinemas, would be outraged with incredulity at the whole affair. A smart-ass 19-year-old passing himself off as a pilot, a lawyer and a doctor while amassing over $2 million through forged cheques? Yeah, right.
  But this is all a relatively faithful adaptation of the autobiography of
10 one Frank Abagnale Jr (co-written with Stan Redding), who did indeed pull off all of the above – and much more besides – before the age of 21. Leonardo DiCaprio plays the con man in question. Early scenes see him honing the art of deception even as an adolescent, posing as a substitute teacher and conducting, rather than joining, a French
15 lesson.
  When his parents announce their intention to divorce, the 17-year-old Abagnale Jr is sent reeling into the big wide world, and so begin his four years of top-level scamming. It's not long before his trickery attracts the attention of the FBI, specifically uptight agent Carl Hanratty
20 (Hanks, turning in a subtly nuanced performance in perhaps his least self-indulgent role, well, ever). Cat-and-mouse shenanigans follow and

17

File   Edit   View   Favorites   Tools   Help

← Back ▾ → ▾ ⊗ ▣ ▵ | ⊘ Search ⬚ Favorites ⬚ Media ⬚ | ▤▾ ▤ ▤▾ ▤

Address ▣ | ▾ ⟳ Go Links »

– would you believe it? – the two build up a grudging respect for one another.

This is not a deeply significant Spielberg movie, but, as anyone who
25   sat through every turgid frame of A.I. can testify, this is not necessarily
a bad thing. What the director does deliver – with the deceptive ease
of an old pro – is a lively caper that is pretty compelling throughout.

Beside the film's breeziness, Spielberg and writer Jeff Nathanson
work in some depth. Abagnale, despite his jet-set lifestyle, cuts a
30   lonely soul. In one scene he telephones Hanratty on Christmas Eve,
ostensibly to taunt him, but in fact – as Hanratty swiftly deduces –
because he's got no one else to talk to. But it's the relationship
between Abagnale and his father, Frank Sr (Christopher Walken), that
provides the film's best moments. Walken is magnificent – rendering
35   Frank Sr outwardly upbeat but with despair oozing out of him as he
tries to maintain dignity in the face of an IRS investigation.

Yet this is all a sideshow to the main event: Abagnale's relentless
scamming. DiCaprio gives a reasonable account of himself in the role,
for the most part coming across as effortlessly charismatic (his
40   teenage girl fan club will love the movie). You can't help wishing for the
dark undertones of, say, John Cusack in The Grifters – after all, when
you think about it, posing as a doctor isn't perhaps as much of a laugh
as it is portrayed here.

Minor gripes aside, what you're left with is a witty, charming comedy-
45   thriller – The Sting for the new millennium (with a jazzy, Mancini-
inspired score by John Williams to boot). It's the sort of film that, if it
were made 50 years ago, people would observe that 'they don't make
'em like this anymore.' Thankfully, courtesy of Mr Spielberg, they do.

incredulity lack of belief
nuanced given a slightly different meaning
turgid inflated
ostensibly seemingly
charismatic magnetic
undertones tones or ideas beneath the surface
to boot as well

Key Reading

Reviews

This text is a **review**. Its **purpose** is to inform and entertain the reader. It also tells us what the reviewer thinks of the film.

The main features of this text are:

● It gives **basic information** about the story line, characters, and the people involved – cast, director, etc, for example, 'A smart-ass 19-year-old passing himself off as a pilot, a lawyer and a doctor.'

● It gives us an idea of what the **reviewer's opinion** is, through the words and phrases selected, for example, 'Minor gripes aside, what you're left with is a witty, charming comedy-thriller.'

● It has a **friendly, informal tone** and uses a number of ways to **'connect' with the reader**, for example, '…would you believe it?'

● It uses a **wide range of sentences** often packed with **detail**, and uses the **present tense**, for example, 'Early scenes *see* him honing the art of deception even as an adolescent…'

1 The names of **three real people** are given in the introductory paragraph – the main actor, the director, and the man the film is based on. Who are they?

2 Find a view expressed by the reviewer in paragraph 4. Which words tell you it is an **opinion** and not a fact?

3 The reviewer talks about the 'cat-and-mouse shenanigans' between the FBI agent and the con man played by DiCaprio. What do you think this means?

Purpose

4 The writer wants to give us a good sense of the feel of the film, and what it is like.

Look at the final paragraph. How does the reviewer **sum up the film**?

Look for an adjective + adjective + noun combination, like this:

> A dull, pointless thriller

Reading for meaning

5 In line 4, why does the reviewer say it is 'fortunate' that this is a **true story**? Discuss these possibilities in pairs:

- because it made a good idea for the story
- because true stories are better than fictional ones
- because it would be too unbelievable if it was made-up.

6 Find any **descriptions** of Frank Abagnale Jr (the con man played by DiCaprio) and note them down. Do you think we are supposed to think of him as a villainous or nasty character? Why?

7 The FBI agent played by Tom Hanks, and Frank's father, played by Christopher Walken, are both described in the review. The agent is described as 'uptight', and the father as 'outwardly upbeat'. What do these descriptions **tell us** about each man?

Focus on: Rhetorical questions

Rhetorical questions are questions that are asked for effect and do not require an answer. There are a number of rhetorical questions in the review. For example:

> A smart-ass 19-year-old passing himself off as a pilot, a lawyer and a doctor while amassing over $2 million through forged cheques? Yeah, right.

Through this question the writer puts himself in the shoes of the audience. He is saying: 'If this wasn't a true story would we believe it?'

A second rhetorical question is used when the reviewer describes how the two men – the agent and the con man – come to respect each other:

> Cat-and-mouse shenanigans follow and – would you believe it? – the two build up a grudging respect for one another.

R12

8 In pairs, **discuss** whether this second question is there because:

- the writer thinks it is surprising
- the writer thinks this happens in lots of films.

Rhetorical questions can be used in lots of ways – for example, to express anger or disgust:

● Are these terrorists really interested in freedom?

● Do you really expect me to forgive you for what you have done?

9 **Complete this rhetorical question** by writing the final part of it:

Police officer to a teenager carrying four mobile phones.

'So, am I supposed to believe that…?'

Key Writing

One of the ways in which the reviewer makes his review interesting is by giving us small glimpses of scenes from the movie. Here, the reviewer describes con man DiCaprio making a call to Tom Hanks:

In one scene he telephones Hanratty on Christmas Eve, ostensibly to taunt him, but in fact – as Hanratty swiftly deduces – because he's got no one else to talk to.

10 Take any scene from a television programme or film you have watched recently.

Then, using the **present tense**, describe what happens in **one sentence**. Try to suggest what it **means**, too. You will need to use:

● precise verbs

● the names of the characters

● a conjunction (for example 'but' or 'although') to link what happens with what this means.

For example:

'In one scene, Paul tries to win Lee back by promising to give up dealing drugs, but we know that he is only faking it – he doesn't really mean it.'

④ Unit 1 Assignment: Story openers

Assessment Focus

▶ **AF6** Write with technical accuracy of syntax and punctuation in phrases, clauses and sentences

---

You: are a writer of detective and mystery stories. A local school has asked you to send in the beginning of one of your best stories for its pupils to finish.

Your task: To write the opening to the story. It can include the detective or the villain, or both. It must also contain some direct speech.

Stage 1

Plan your opening. Make brief notes about your main character's appearance – include strong adjectives.

- Name
- Face
- Build (stocky, slim, etc.)
- Clothing
- Any other important details (you don't have to use them in your story – they can just be background information)

Also plan:

Where the story begins. For example, in a modern flat? On a station platform? On a rooftop?

What happens in your opening, for example, the detective gets a visit to their flat late one night.

Stage 2

Draft your **first paragraph**.

● Make sure you describe **what your character is doing** clearly. Use your notes to tell the reader what your character **looks like**.

● Write in the **past tense** using the **third person**.

For example:

'Inspector Mortimer *answered* the door.
In front of him *stood* a tall man holding a gun.'

Stage 3

Think about how you can use **dialogue** in your other paragraphs, and what your characters might say. Use a mixture of direct and indirect speech to add variety to your writing.

Then draft at least **three more paragraphs**.

Grammar for reading

Direct speech is the words that are actually spoken by characters. Speech marks are placed around the spoken words, and a new line is started for each speaker. Punctuation linked to what is said goes *before* the last speech mark, for example: ' "Come in," said Inspector Mortimer, coolly.'
Indirect speech is when words are reported; the actual spoken words are not used. No speech marks are needed, for example: 'Inspector Mortimer told the man that he could come into the flat.'

Challenge

Make your opening even more interesting by using more than one narrator. Try writing one paragraph as if narrated by the detective character, the next as if narrated by the villain/criminal.

Narrator One:

'I answered the door. In front of me stood a tall, pale man holding a gun.'

Narrator Two:

'I entered the room, noticing that the normally cool Mortimer was shaking slightly. I had him rattled.'

① How words are formed

Aims

▶ Read an explanation text

▶ Discuss the process it describes (S&L2)

▶ Examine how it creates tone

▶ Express your own opinions

Read the following extract from Bill Bryson's book about the English Language, *Mother Tongue*. In this section, he is discussing how words are formed.

WORDS ARE CREATED BY ADDING OR SUBTRACTING SOMETHING.

English has more than a hundred common prefixes and suffixes *-able, -ness, -ment, -pre, -dis, -anti* and so on – and with these it can form and re-form words with a facility that yet again sets it apart from other tongues. For example, we can take the French word *mutin* (rebellion)
5   and turn it into *mutiny, mutinous, mutinously, mutineer* and many others, while the French have still just the one form, *mutin*.

      Some word endings are surprisingly rare. If you think of *angry* and *hungry*, you might conclude that *-gry* is a common ending, but in fact it occurs in no other common words in English. Similarly *-dous* appears in
10   only *stupendous, horrendous, tremendous, hazardous* and *jeopardous*, while *-lock* survives only in *wedlock* and *warlock* and *-red* only in *hatred* and *kindred*. *Forgiveness* is the only example of a verb + *-ness* form. Equally some common seeming prefixes are actually more rare than superficial thought might lead us to conclude. If you think of *forgive,*
15   *forget, forgo, forbid, forbear, forlorn, forsake* and *forswear*, you might think that *for-* is a common prefix, but in fact it appears in no other

common words, though once it appeared in scores of others. Why certain forms like -ish, -ness, -ful and -some should continue to thrive while others like -lock and -gry that were once equally popular should fall into
20   disuse is a question without a good answer.

Fashion clearly has something to do with it. The suffix -dom was long in danger of disappearing, except in a few established words like kingdom, but it underwent a resurgence (largely instigated in America) in the last century, giving us such useful locutions as officialdom and
25   boredom and later more contrived forms like best-sellerdom. The ending -en is today one of the most versatile ways we have of forming verbs from adjectives (harden, loosen, sweeten, etc.) and yet almost all such words are less than 300 years old.

The process is still perhaps the most prolific way of forming new
30   words and often the simplest. For centuries we had the word political, but by loading the single letter a onto the front of it, a new word, apolitical, joined the language in 1952.

Still other words are formed by lopping off their ends. Mob, for example, is a shortened form of mobile vulgus (fickle crowd). Exam, gym,
35   and lab are similar truncations, all of them dating only from the last century when syllabic amputations were the rage. Yet the impulse to shorten words is an ancient one. Indeed, many of our most common words are contractions of whole phrases – for instance, goodbye, a shortening of God-be-with-you, and hello, which was in Old English hal
40   beo thu or 'whole be thou'.

Finally, but no less importantly, English possesses the ability to make new words by fusing compounds – airport, seashore, footwear, wristwatch, landmark, flowerpot and so on almost endlessly. All Indo-European languages have the capacity to form compounds. Indeed,
45   German and Dutch do it, one might say, to excess. But English does it more neatly than most other languages, eschewing the choking word chains that bedevil other Germanic languages and employing the nifty refinement of making the elements reversible, so that we can distinguish between a houseboat and a boathouse, between basketwork and a
50   workbasket, between a casebook and a bookcase. Other languages lack this facility.

---

superficial not very deep
locutions words
resurgence a comeback
apolitical not interested in politics
syllabic amputations cutting off parts of words
Indo-European the language family to which English belongs
eschewing avoiding

Key Reading

Explanation texts

This is an **explanation** text. Its **purpose** is to explain how a process works in an entertaining manner.

The main features of this text are:

- It has a series of **clear and logical steps** which may include a topic sentence to introduce each step, for example, 'Some word endings are surprisingly rare.'

- It uses **examples** to illustrate the point being explained, such as 'Forgiveness is the only example of a verb + -ness form.'

- It uses **sentence signposts** to organise and link points clearly, for example, '*Still* other words are formed…'

- It uses the **present tense**, when the text is explaining how or why something is now, for example, 'the French *have* still just the one form, mutin.'

- It uses **precise vocabulary**, including technical terms which may be explained in a glossary, for example, 'All *Indo-European* languages have the capacity to form *compounds*.'

1 a) Identify the **topic sentence** that presents the main point in paragraph 3.

b) How does this **link back** to paragraph 2?

2 Find an example of a sentence written in the **past tense**. Why is this tense used at this point?

3 Some of the examples in the text give **unexpected information** about familiar words. Choose two examples of this.

4 Look through the glossary. **How many** of the words listed did you need to look up as you read the text?

. . . .

Purpose

The purpose of this text is to explain and to entertain. The challenge of writing it is that it is telling the reader about something they are already familiar with – their own language.

Wr7

5 In pairs, discuss how well the text both explains and entertains. Consider how Bryson:

● provides **unusual examples**

● reveals **surprising things** that we might not have thought about

● uses **playful comments**.

. . . .

Reading for meaning

S11

6 a) As well as the use of prefixes and suffixes, name the two other **word-forming processes** that are presented in the extract.

b) In **which paragraphs** does Bryson introduce each of these processes?

7 a) What is the **mystery** about some prefixes and suffixes?

b) Read paragraphs 2 and 3 again, this time listing the **examples** provided under two headings:

Prefixes/suffixes found in many words	Prefixes/suffixes only found in a few words

Be careful not to confuse *commonly used* with *used in many words*.

8 Of the three word-forming processes explained, which one produces the **most** words? Which paragraph makes this clear?

9 What is clever about the way in which English **compound words** work?

· ·

Focus on: Tone

One of the risks of writing an explanation that is packed full of information is that it can be rather 'dry'. In order to make it more interesting, Bill Bryson has added an element of commentary to his explanation. This involves two main techniques:

● He makes remarks to suggest that English is superior to other European languages.

● He shows his admiration for the English language.

10 Note down **examples** from the text where Bill Bryson shows that English is better than:

Wr7

● French

● other Germanic languages.

11 In pairs, go through the text and collect examples of Bryson's **positive statements** about English. Record your findings in a table like the one below:

Statement	What it shows about the author's attitude
'it can form and re-form words with a facility that yet again sets it apart from other tongues'	He thinks English forms words more easily than other languages.

12 Look closely at the following words in bold, taken from lines 46–48. In this case, Bryson interweaves his comments as he explains one of his points:

> …eschewing the **choking** word **chains** that **bedevil** other Germanic languages and employing the **nifty refinement** of making the elements reversible…

a) What does Bill Bryson's choice of words here show about his attitude to **'other Germanic' languages**?

b) What does his choice of words here show about his attitude to **English**?

13 Do you think Bill Bryson makes these remarks because:

- he genuinely believes them
- he wants to draw comparisons between European languages
- he wishes to flatter English readers
- he believes there will be few French or German readers.

Explain your choices with **evidence** from the extract.

14 In pairs, **discuss** whether you think Bryson's enthusiasm works. Do you feel more positive about English after reading this passage? Or do you feel the other languages have been misrepresented?

Key Writing

The challenge of writing about language is that readers may believe they already know what you are telling them, so the way the explanation is presented becomes more important.

15 a) In pairs, **look at the key facts** given below to explain 'why we have day and night'.

● Earth rotates round the Sun once per year.

● Earth rotates on its own axis once every 24 hours.

● Day is when Earth faces the Sun.

● Night is when we are in Earth's own shadow.

Discuss **how you would present an explanation** of these facts as interestingly and enthusiastically as possible to an audience of people of your own age? Think about:

● your **choice of language** – include a *few* comments on the facts you are introducing

● your **ordering of the main points** and how you will link them – use causal language and sentence signposts

● your **choice of examples** – select the most interesting.

b) Write your brief explanation. You could begin:

The miracle of day and night is not often appreciated, especially by those of us who can't get up in the morning.

② Online words

Aims

▶ Read an information text

▶ Discuss the ideas it raises (S11)

▶ Examine methods of structure and presentation (Wr7)

▶ Express your own opinions (S&L9)

Read the following newspaper article about the role of the Internet in the development of the English Language

ONLINE WORDS TAKE WING

Our vocabulary is constantly being enriched, but the web is now accelerating the process. Robbie Hudson hails a new word order.

New things have always needed naming, of course, and 'googling', 'blog' and 'fanfic' are essentially phenomena of the internet rather than indications of any great transformation of the language. Indeed, Eric S. Raymond, the presiding eminence at *The Jargon File* (www.catb.org/~esr/jargon), a dictionary devoted to the vocabulary of the techie community, doubts that there has been an increase in linguistic ingenuity, but he adds that 'pre-internet, a much higher percentage was never captured in any equivalent of an archive'.

This is crucial because, for a word to enter the language permanently, it must be written down. The OED [Oxford English Dictionary] website notes that of the many words credited to Shakespeare, some were terms he was merely the first person to record in a form that has survived. The web is revolutionising how this happens today by disseminating new words at lightning speed and storing them in searchable archives.

Fiona McPherson, a senior editor at the OED who deals with new words, explains that she has to be enormously careful because, 'once a word makes the dictionary, it is there for ever'. She adds that the dictionary is not a comprehensive list of all words ever used, because language is a living thing. 'As soon as anyone uses a new word to communicate, it is part of the language, but we aim to include all words that achieve a degree of permanency.'

The internet is an intrinsically verbal medium, and full of people who are fascinated by words. As well as such dictionaries as *The Jargon File*, there are dozens of sites devoted to spotting neologisms – one of the best being *The Word Spy*, which Fiona McPherson certainly keeps in her sights. She also refers to web databases to find words she can follow to printed records (OED editors are extremely unhappy about citing online sources that might disappear at the flick of a switch).

In addition, the number of times a word appears in a search engine gives a rough guide to how widely it is used, though this is a blunt instrument and might simply show that one substantial source is keen on that word; McPherson explains that words generally merit consideration only when they achieve both breadth (typically five separate written sources) and endurance (typically five years).

In pre-internet times, compiling a new edition of the OED was such a herculean undertaking that only two have been published in 75 years – along with a few volumes of additions. Inevitably, some words slipped through the cracks. The online version has made updating easier, with something like 200 words added every quarter. The editors' standards have not dropped a jot, but the explosion of archives online means that words used by quite private groups have become more permanent and widespread.

[George Bush's] use of 'misunderestimate' has a chance of making the OED because the dictionary is descriptive, not prescriptive. It is the historical record of a living language, and, as Jesse Sheidlower of the OED points out: 'We are not the Académie Française. The internet, which spreads misunderstandings as quickly as everything else, helps to solidify misusage as well as usage. If a speech by the president of the USA, who has degrees from Harvard and Yale, isn't indicative of use, then what is?'

Giving new words permanency enriches the language.

googling searching the internet using the 'Google' search engine

blog short for 'web log' – a form of on-line diary

fanfic short for 'fan fiction' – continuations of well known books by fans

phenomena occurences arising from

presiding eminence head

techie community people interested in technology

archive a form of storage

disseminating spreading

intrinsically essentially, basically

neologisms new word

herculean very difficult (like one of the twelve tasks of Hercules)

prescriptive in this context, a dictionary that tells how words ought to be used

descriptive in this context, a dictionary that tells how words are actually used

Académie Française a French committee responsible for keeping the French language 'pure'

Key Reading

Information texts

This is an **information** text. Its **purpose** is to inform the reader about something.

The main features of this text are:

● It contains both **general statements** and **specific facts**, for example, '…for a word to enter the language permanently, it must be written down'.

● It uses the **present tense** when telling things as they are now, for example, 'The internet is an intrinsically verbal medium…'

● It uses **specialist vocabulary**, for example, 'descriptive, not prescriptive…'

● It uses **formal** and **impersonal language**, for example, '…we aim to include all words that achieve a degree of permanency.'

1 Why do you think there are so many words from paragraph 2 in the **glossary**?

S11 **2** Identify three words in this text that you think **did not exist** ten years ago.

3 Find a rare example of the **past tense** in paragraph 7. Why has it been used here?

4 Which words and phrases make the following sentence both **formal** and **impersonal**?

In pre-internet times, compiling a new edition of the OED was such a herculean undertaking that only two have been published in 75 years…

Purpose

5 In pairs, discuss what you think the **main purpose** of this text is:

- to inform the reader about new words entering the language
- to help the reader to understand how new words become permanent
- to give information about how the Internet is speeding up the process of entry of new words into the language.

Provide **evidence** for your choice from the text.

6 Decide together who the **main audience** is for this text:

- the on-line techie community
- readers of this newspaper in general
- language specialists.

What clues in the text support your decision?

Reading for meaning

7 **a)** What must **happen** to a new word before it can enter the English language permanently?

b) **How long** do dictionary makers wait before they decide a word is permanent? And **how many** written sources do they require?

8 In your own words explain how the **Internet** is of help to dictionary makers.

9 In pairs, look back at each paragraph of the text and find the **key words** or **topic sentence**. Write these down.

10 Use these topic sentences in a **spidergram** to show the shape of the text. Follow the example begun below:

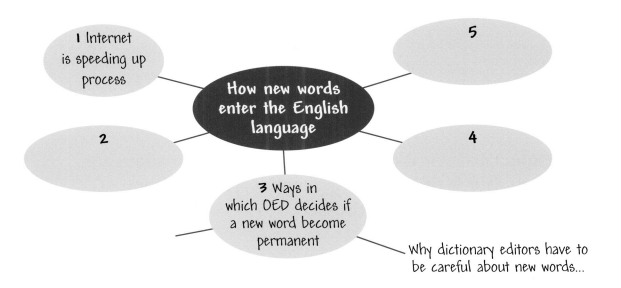

1 Internet is speeding up process

How new words enter the English language

5

2

4

3 Ways in which OED decides if a new word become permanent

Why dictionary editors have to be careful about new words...

You will notice that each main point may be covered by one paragraph or by several in the text.

Focus on: Specialist vocabulary

Every subject area has its own specialist vocabulary. In some subjects this is very obvious.

11 Can you identify the subject areas that these words belong to?
   a) Chemotherapy
   b) Highest common factor
   c) Erosion
   d) Inertia
   e) Monotheism

In other areas, the specialist vocabulary is less obvious. In English-language studies, for example, 'word' could be seen as a specialist term.

12 Fill in the table below with examples of **specialist vocabulary** from different areas and their ordinary meanings.

Word	Ordinary meaning	Specialist meaning	Area of knowledge
hard drive			ICT
mass			physics
sum			maths
sentence			criminology
entry			dictionaries
bug			ICT

Using specialist vocabulary is fine when your readers are specialists, but it causes problems when an audience of non-specialists is being addressed.

13 In pairs, look again at the specialist terms in paragraph 2 of the extract. How many did you know **without checking them** in the glossary?

The most common way of providing help with specialist vocabulary is to provide explanations as you go along. For example:

> Erosion (the gradual wearing away of rock by wind and water) helps to shape the landscape.

One potential problem with this is that the explanations can start to get in the way of understanding the basic information.

14 With a partner, discuss whether bracketed explanations or glossaries are the **best method** for helping a reader with specialist terms.

Wr7

Key Writing

There is a famous story of how the word 'quiz' came about. Two men had a bet to see if they could introduce a new word into English. They decided on the word 'quiz' for their experiment, and the one man had it written up on walls around Dublin. People naturally asked what this word meant and thus began the modern meaning of the word.

15 Using the information you have gained from the text, **write an article aimed at teenagers** on how they can get one of their favourite, but little-known words, into the dictionary.

In pairs, **brainstorm** ideas for your information text. Choose your word carefully: it should be either useful or original (for example, a word used by skateboarders or a word used by a group of friends).

Then summarise your main points in a spidergram like the one below.

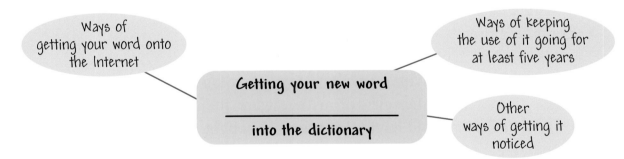

b) On your own, decide how you will **split your main points into paragraphs**. One point could make one or two paragraphs.

c) Write your short information text, remembering to:
- write in the **present tense**
- use **formal language** but also include some **informal phrases** (remember your audience)
- use some **specialist vocabulary** (decide which terms need explaining).

③ Punctuation makes sense

Aims

◗ Read an extract from a argument text
◗ Develop the skill of looking for key ideas
◗ Look at the author's use of emotive language (R12)
◗ Write your own argument

Read the following text. It is from the introduction to the best-selling book about punctuation, *Eats, Shoots and Leaves*. Here, the author, Lynne Truss, explains how she became obsessed with words and punctuation.

While other girls were out with boyfriends on Sunday afternoons, getting their necks disfigured by love bites, I was at home with the wireless listening to an Ian Messiter quiz called *Many a Slip*, in which erudite and amusing contestants spotted

5 grammatical errors in pieces of prose. It was a fantastic programme. I dream sometimes they have brought it back. Panellists such as Isobel Barnett and David Nixon would interrupt Roy Plomley with a buzz and say 'Tautology!' Around this same time, when other girls of my age were attending the

10 Isle of Wight Festival and having abortions, I bought a copy of Eric Partridge's *Usage and Abusage* and covered it in sticky-backed plastic so that it would last a lifetime (it has). Funny how I didn't think any of this was peculiar at the time, when it was behaviour with 'Proto Stickler' written all over it.

15 But I do see now why it was no accident that I later wound up as a sub-editor with a literal blue pencil.

But to get back to those dark-side-of-the-moon years in British education when teachers upheld the view that grammar and spelling got in the way of self-expression, it is arguable that the

20 timing of their grammatical apathy could not have been worse. In the 1970s, no educationist would have predicted the explosion in universal written communication caused by the personal computer, the internet and the key-pad of the mobile phone. But now, look what's happened: everyone's a writer! Everyone is posting film reviews on Amazon that go like this:

25 I watched this film [*About a Boy*] a few days ago expecting the usual hugh Grant bumbling ... character Ive come to loathe/expect over the years. i was thoroughly suprised. This film was great, one of the best films i have seen in a long time. The film focuses around one man who starts going to a

30 single parents meeting, to meet women, one problem He doesnt have a child.

Isn't this sad? People who have been taught nothing about their own language are (contrary to educational expectations) spending all their leisure hours attempting to string sentences together for

35 the edification of others. And there is no editing on the internet! Meanwhile, in the world of text messages, ignorance of grammar and punctuation obviously doesn't affect a person's ability to communicate messages such as 'C U later'. But if you try anything longer, it always seems to turn out much like the writing

40 of the infant Pip in *Great Expectations*:

MI DEER JO I OPE U R KRWITE WELL I OPE I SHAL SON B HABELL 4 2 TEEDGE U JO AN THEN WE SHORL B SO GLODD AN WEN I M PRENGTD 2 U JO WOT LARX AN BLEVE ME INF XN PIP.

---

erudite clever and well read

wireless an old-fashioned term for radio

tautology saying the same thing in a slightly different way – for example, return back home

Usage and Abusage a famous book on correct English usage

apathy lack of interest

Proto Stickler someone who is going to become a stickler (for correct language)

blue pencil the colour of pencil used by editors to mark mistakes

Great Expectations A novel by Charles Dickens – the quotation is from when Pip is learning to write

Key Reading

Argument texts

This is an **argument** text. Its **purpose** is to convince the reader of a particular point of view.

The main features of this text are:

- It presents a **series of points** backed up by **reasons or evidence**, for example, the point about the Internet causing more people to write, is backed up by an example of an Internet film review.

- It uses **topic sentences** to introduce each main point, for example, 'While other girls were out with boyfriends… I was at home with the wireless …'

- It uses **formal** language but with some **informal** language for effect, for example, 'No educationist would have predicted…' and 'Funny how I didn't think any of this was peculiar…'

- It uses a mainly **reasonable tone** but occasionally a **highly emotive** one, for example, 'Isn't this sad?' and 'attending the Isle of Wight Festival and having abortions…'

1 Identify the **topic sentence** in paragraph 2. Remember, topic sentences do not always come early in the paragraph.

2 This text contains a mixture of formal and informal language. **Find one example of each**.

3 What **attitude** to British education in the 1970s does the author show when she calls that era the 'dark-side-of-the-moon years'?

4 How is the author trying to affect the **reader's feelings** when she asks the question 'Isn't this sad?' How would the effect be different if she had written 'Isn't this bad?'

· ·

Purpose

The purpose of this text is to argue for greater attention to spelling and grammar. It does this with a combination of personal statements and more formal arguments.

R11

5 In pairs, discuss how the writer **presents herself** in the personal statements.

● Does she seem better or worse than the girls she grew up with?

● Is her interest in grammar made to sound exciting or slightly sad?

S10

6 Consider how well the writer's argument about grammar **works**.

● Do you think there is more 'writing' in everyday life now than in the 1970s?

● Do you think people need to improve their written expression because of this?

Be prepared to report your ideas back to the class.

· ·

Reading for meaning

7 Does paragraph 1 tell the reader **more** about:

● what Lynne Truss was interested in the 1960s

● what the general interest in grammar was in the 1960s?

8 What **reason** is given in paragraph 2 for why grammar and spelling were not taught in the 1970s?

9 What **developments** have happened since to make grammar and spelling more important?

10 What piece of **evidence** is used to support the writer's argument that spelling and grammar are important in longer text messages?

. . . .

Focus on: Emotive language

Although her argument is logical, the writer's personal feelings about correct grammar and spelling are also made very plain.

11 a) In pairs, look through the extract and make a list of as many **positive statements** about language as you can.

b) Now make a list of some of the **negative statements**.

c) Who or **what** are the negative statements applied to?

12 What do the two main pieces of evidence **suggest** about people who don't care about grammar and spelling?

R12 **13** Consider each of the statements in the table below. Then **complete column 2** to suggest how each is meant to affect the reader's feelings.

Statement from argument	How it is meant to affect the reader
'Girls … getting their necks disfigured by love bites'	
'erudite and amusing contestants spotted grammatical errors'	
'other girls of my age were attending the Isle of Wight Festival and having abortions'	
'covered it in sticky-backed plastic so that it would last a lifetime (it has)'	
'the timing of their grammatical apathy could not have been worse'	
'People … spending all their leisure hours attempting to string sentences together'	
'like the writing of the infant Pip'	

Key Writing

14 Your task is to **write a letter** to a music magazine in which you argue that the pop charts do not reflect the best music.

a) Begin by **brainstorming** your main arguments in small groups.

b) On your own, select from your brainstorm the **three main arguments** you will use. Try to **add reasons or evidence** alongside to support them. Part of your plan might look like this:

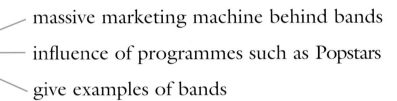

Chart-topping music is all hype

massive marketing machine behind bands

influence of programmes such as Popstars

give examples of bands

c) **Draft your letter**, remembering to:

- invent the name of the person you are writing to (for example, Dear DJ Whiz…)

- use a reasonable tone to put across your main points

- highlight key points and reasons with emotive language to make your feelings clear.

(4) Unit 2 Assignment: Magazine writer

Assessment Focus

▶ AF2 Produce texts which are appropriate to task, reader and purpose

You: are a magazine columnist.

Your task: to write an argument explaining that English is not getting worse – it is just changing with the times, aimed at older readers who complain about declining standards of English.

Stage 1

Think carefully about the **content** of your argument. Here are some ideas to help you generate your main points:

● English has always changed; for example, Britain has been invaded time and time again; new continents discovered and new words brought back by explorers.

● The language is always reinventing itself – new words are formed through change and suffixes/prefixes.

● Changes still happening – advance of technology; speed with which new words are being thought up and taken up on internet/mobile phones/e-mail.

● Best way is to adapt to these changes – then they won't seem so bad.

● How the language is protected – by the makers of dictionaries and editors.

● Is there anything to worry about? Project to the future: how might the language change further?

Use ideas and examples from the texts on pages 26 and 33 to add reasons and pieces of evidence for each of your arguments. For example:

Language is constantly changing: the Old English greeting 'Whole be thou' has morphed in the last 1000 years into our 'Hello'. There is no reason for these changes to stop...

Stage 2

Consider your **audience** and how you might **influence their views** by using emotive language.

- What sort of things would appeal to your audience? (For example, taking pride in the language; using spelling and punctuation accurately.)
- How do you show that you understand their feelings? (For example, with reassuring words.)
- How do you make them change their ideas? (For example, by using positive phrases about recent changes to the language.)

Add these ideas to your plan.

Stage 3

Draft your article, using your plan, but adding any new ideas or phrases that occur to you as you write.

Remember to:
- include a topic sentence in each paragraph to signal a new point or idea
- keep your tone reasonable most of the time
- use emotive language occasionally to help convince your audience
- match the formality of your language to your older audience.

Influential voices

① Elvis the King

Aims

▸ Read a passage about Elvis Presley

▸ Explore how non-fiction texts can entertain the audience (Wr7)

▸ Explain why your own favourite singer is so great (Wr10)

This is the opening passage of a book about Elvis Presley, the 'King' of rock and roll by Frank Coffey.

ELVIS: Why We Love Him, Why We Study Him

Elvis is called 'the King' because he was the flashpoint, the linchpin, the centrepiece of a musical and cultural revolution called rock and roll. It can be said that the rock revolution went on to become the most significant worldwide cultural phenomenon of the 20th century,
5   affecting style, language, art, film, customs, values, ethics, as well as music. Elvis Presley started the revolution.

Elvis Presley made musical and social history by combining heretofore primarily black forms of music – rhythm and blues (R 'n' B) and gospel – with primarily white forms of music – country-western and pop – to
10 create a whole new thing called rock.

Of course, Elvis wasn't the only singer bringing rock to the mass American audience. But it was Elvis Presley, preternaturally handsome, sneeringly sexy, with a voice both raw and velvety, who captured the hearts and minds (and loins) of mainstream America. Elvis started out
15 as a pretender to the throne and became the King.

Need another way to get a handle on the King? Think of The Beatles.

Like Elvis, the boys from Liverpool (who were huge Elvis fans – even idolisers) radically changed music and culture. Girls
20 swooned, parents raged. Elvis gave us pompadours and sideburns; The Beatles, long locks and facial hair. Elvis was rebellion, '50s style: fast cars and hot nights. The Beatles provided the late '60s/early '70s version: peace, love and
25 consciousness alteration. But they shared one thing: impact. It's not too grandiose to say that everyone in America was affected by Elvis and The Beatles. Everyone. But Elvis was first.

Elvis died early, at age 42. And, subsequently, something highly improbable happened to Elvis Aaron Presley: the King
30 became bigger in death than in life. Today, Elvis is ubiquitous. A million fans make an annual pilgrimage to his Memphis home, Graceland. Elvis made more money in the
35 three years after his death than during his entire career. He has sold over one billion records.

In the beginning, there was Elvis. The father of a generation's music. To know him is to know the most influential art form of the 20th century
40 – rock and roll. To understand him is to understand the country: innocent and calculating, vibrant and vulnerable, powerful and flawed – envied and admired around the world.

Elvis Presley left this life in 1977 at age 42. But he will never die.

Long live the King.

THE KING AND I

"Before Elvis, there was nothing."
– John Lennon

THE KING AND I

"There have been contenders, but there is only one King."
– Bruce Springsteen

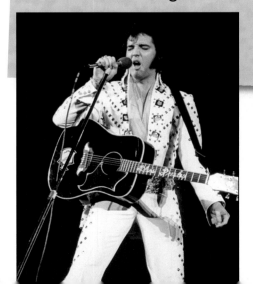

linchpin key player

phenomenon remarkable event

heretofore until this time, up to that point

preternaturally unusually

pompadour a hairstyle: long hair brushed up and back from the forehead

consciousness alteration changing how you see the world (through drugs)

ubiquitous everywhere

Key Reading

Explanation texts

This is an **explanation** text. Its **purpose** is to explain how or why something is as it is.

The main features of this text are:

- Its **form** is a series of **logical steps** explaining why something is the case. For example, the first sentence makes a statement about Elvis' huge importance.

- It uses **causal language**, for example, 'Elvis is called the King *because* he was the flashpoint…of a musical and cultural revolution.'

- It contains a mixture of **present** and **past tense**, depending on the focus, for example, 'Elvis *is called* the King' – present tense; 'Elvis Presley *made* musical and social history' – past tense.

- It uses mainly **formal language**, for example, 'the most significant worldwide cultural phenomenon of the 20th century.'

1 Paragraph 2 gives more detail about how Elvis was the centrepiece of the rock and roll revolution. Why has the author put this paragraph **here**?

2 a) What **point** does the author make in the first sentence of paragraph 3? What point is made in the second sentence?

b) What is the **link** between these two sentences? What **connective** does the author use to make this link clear?

3 In paragraph 5, identify two verbs in the **present tense** and two in the **past tense**. Explain why both tenses have been used.

4 'And, subsequently, something highly improbable happened to Elvis.' (lines 28–30)
Reword this formal statement using **informal language**.

Purpose

5 In pairs, discuss whether the **main purpose** of this text is:

● to show how Elvis is greater than The Beatles
● to explain why Elvis is such an important figure
● to give us basic information about Elvis Presley.

Use **causal language** to explain your reasons.

Reading for meaning

6 Give **two reasons** why, according to the author, Elvis is so important.

7 'Elvis started out as a pretender to the throne and became the King' (lines 14–15).
What does the author **mean** by this?

8 Elvis Presley 'will never die' (line 43). **Why not**?

9 What is the **purpose** of the sidebars ('The King and I')? Are they effective?

Dashes are used in two main ways in the text:
● **one dash** can extend a sentence – like this
● **two dashes** can interrupt a sentence – like this – before carrying on.

10 a) Find **one example** of each type of dash in the text.

b) How could the author have punctuated these sentences **differently**?

· ·

Focus on: An entertaining style

The author has a rich **vocabulary** and an exciting style. The result is a text that entertains as well as explains. In this section we will look at some of the author's techniques.

Powerful words

The author uses interesting words where possible. This ensures that his writing is never dull.

Wr7 **11** Which of the words in the box are **nearest in meaning** to:

a) grandiose   **b)** improbable?

> unbelievable   fantastic   unlikely
>   big-headed   exaggerated

Powerful phrases

Sometimes two words can work together to make a powerful phrase:

'sneeringly sexy'

- links the adjectives 'sneering' and 'sexy' by making one of them into an adverb – 'sneeringly' instead of 'sneering'
- the alliteration of 's' adds impact

'vibrant and vulnerable'

- two words describing very different characteristics – bringing them together is unusual and powerful
- the alliteration of 'v' adds impact

12 **Choose two words** from the list below to make one effective phrase describing someone. It may help to turn one of the words into an adverb. Explain why your phrase is **effective**.

> crazy   casual   close   chaotic   controlled
> controversial   clinging   careful

Key Writing

Wr10

13 **a) Discuss** with a partner who you think is the **best singer or band today**. Try to give reasons for your choice.

b) Each **write some notes** on your chosen singer or band. Use some of the ideas that came up in your discussion.

c) Use these notes to **draft a paragraph** for your school magazine. The heading is: 'Why …………… is the best'.

- Start by giving the reader some basic information about your singer.

- Give at least two reasons why they are the best at what they do. Remember to use causal language ('because', 'as a result').

- Use powerful words and phrases.

53

② God bless Africa!

Aims

▶ Read the final part of a speech by Nelson Mandela

▶ Analyse the use of rhetorical devices in the speech (R12)

▶ Use Standard English to present your findings to the class (S&L2)

Nelson Mandela was released from prison in 1990. This is the final part of the speech that he gave in 1994, when he was sworn in as the first black president of South Africa.

The time for the healing of the wounds has come. The moment to bridge the chasms that divide us has come. The time to build is upon us. We have, at last, achieved our political emancipation. We pledge ourselves to
5 liberate all our people from the continuing bondage of poverty, deprivation, suffering, gender and other discrimination.

We succeeded in taking our last steps to freedom in conditions of relative peace. We commit ourselves to the
10 construction of a complete, just and lasting peace. We have triumphed in the effort to implant hope in the breasts of the millions of our people. We enter into a covenant that we shall build the society in which all South Africans, both black and white, will be able to
15 walk tall, without any fear in their hearts, assured of their inalienable right to human dignity – a rainbow nation at peace with itself and the world.

…We dedicate this day to all the heroes and heroines in this country and the rest of the world who sacrificed in
20 many ways and surrendered their lives so that we could be free. Their dreams have become reality. Freedom is their reward.

25 We are both humbled and elevated by the honour and privilege that you, the people of South Africa, have bestowed on us, as the first President of a united, democratic, non-racial and non-sexist government. We understand it still that there is no easy road to freedom. We know it well that none of us acting alone can achieve success. We must therefore act together as a united

30 people, for national reconciliation, for nation building, for the birth of a new world.

Let there be justice for all. Let there be peace for all. Let there be work, bread, water and salt for all. Let each know that for each the body, the mind and the soul have

35 been freed to fulfil themselves. Never, never and never again shall it be that this beautiful land will again experience the oppression of one by another and suffer the indignity of being the skunk of the world. Let freedom reign. The sun shall never set on so glorious a

40 human achievement!

God bless Africa!

chasm	huge gap, gulf
emancipation	freedom
pledge	promise
covenant	solemn agreement
inalienable	absolute

Key Reading

Persuasion texts

This is a **persuasion** text. Its **purpose** is to win the audience over to the speaker's message.

The main features of this text are:

- It presents a **single viewpoint** supported by a **series of points**. For example, Mandela begins by making the point that this is a critical time.

- It uses **emotive language**, for example, 'Let there be peace for all.'

- It uses **powerful imagery** to draw a picture in the audience's mind, for example, 'a *rainbow* nation at peace with itself and the world.'

- It uses **rhetorical techniques** to help get the message across, for example, '*Never, never* and *never* again.'

1 What **point** does Mandela make in the third paragraph?

2 Emotive words are words that are guaranteed to make you feel something. Mandela uses some simple words, like 'peace', which has a lot of meaning and feeling behind it. Find **two other emotive words** in the speech and explain your choice.

3 What picture does 'a rainbow nation' draw? Explain why it is an **effective image**.

Purpose

4 In this speech, Mandela gives his audience a vision of the future of South Africa.

    a) Find at least four **wishes or promises** he makes for the future.

    b) What are the four or five **key words or phrases** in this vision? Sketch an outline map of South Africa and write these key words in it.

South
Africa

5 Mandela is careful not to celebrate a black victory over white.

    a) Find **three places** where he emphasises the triumph of all the people of South Africa.

    b) Why do you think he does this? Is it **effective**?

Reading for meaning

6 The swearing in of a new president is a very formal occasion. It therefore demands formal language in the president's speech. Point to **two features** that make this sentence formal:

> We are both humbled and elevated by the honour and privilege that you, the people of South Africa, have bestowed on us.

7 Mandela promises that South Africa will never again be the 'skunk of the world' (line 38). This refers to the decades before democracy, when apartheid (a system where black people and white people were kept apart) was in force.

Explain why this image has been used. How **effective** is it?

8 In groups of five, prepare a reading of this speech. Focus on:
- emphasising the **key words**
- **pausing** at key points
- varying the **volume** of your delivery.

• •

Focus on: Rhetorical techniques

Rhetorical techniques are used to persuade an audience. Here are four rhetorical techniques used by Mandela in his speech:

Repetition Repeating the same word, phrase or sentence structure hammers the point home. For example: 'Let there be justice for all. Let there be peace for all.'	**Making a list** Listing different examples of the same thing emphasises the point and builds up momentum. For example: '...*the body, the mind and the soul* have been freed...'
Using personal pronouns Using 'you' engages with the audience directly. Using 'I' or 'we' includes the audience on the speaker's side. For example: '*We* pledge *ourselves* to liberate all *our* people.'	**Sound devices** Using sound effects, such as alliteration or rhyme, makes the point sound more attractive. For example: 'We *c*ommit ourselves to the *c*onstruction of a *c*omplete, just and lasting peace.'

R12

9 Look through Mandela's speech in groups. **Identify the rhetorical techniques** that he has used and discuss what effect they have. Draw up a table like the one below to record your findings.

Example	Rhetorical technique	Effect
'Let there be justice for all. Let there be peace for all.' (line 32)	repetition, sound effect	Very strong repetition – only one word different in each case. Puts the point across well.
'the body, the mind and the soul' (line 34)	list	Builds up the picture of all parts of us.

Key Speaking and Listening

10 Your task is to make a **formal presentation** to the class, of the rhetoric in Mandela's speech. Working in pairs:

● Explain what rhetorical techniques are, and what they are for.

● Choose one example of each rhetorical technique, show how it works, and how effective it is in your view.

● Compare one example with a rewritten version of your own that does not use that technique. For example:

'The time for the healing of wounds has come. The moment to bridge the chasms that divide us has come' – the repetition of the sentence structure gives the opening a powerful rhythm. This is much better than, 'The time for the healing of wounds has come, and we must bridge the chasms that divide us.'

● Remember to make your presentation in standard english. Imagine that this is a formal occasion – discuss with your partner how you can make your language and presentation as formal as possible.

Writing to a celeb

Aims

▶ Read some advice for young people on how to get a celebrity to help with a campaign

▶ Evaluate the presentational devices used in the text (Wr4)

▶ Write and present the next section of advice (Wr15)

The following is part of a 'campaigning toolkit' website for young people.

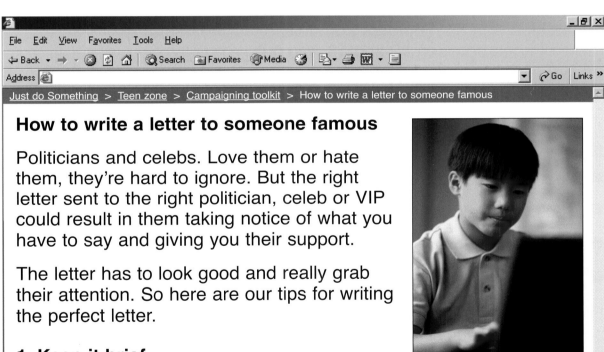

Just do Something > Teen zone > Campaigning toolkit > How to write a letter to someone famous

How to write a letter to someone famous

Politicians and celebs. Love them or hate them, they're hard to ignore. But the right letter sent to the right politician, celeb or VIP could result in them taking notice of what you have to say and giving you their support.

The letter has to look good and really grab their attention. So here are our tips for writing the perfect letter.

1. Keep it brief

Try to write no more than 300 words. The person you write to may get hundreds of letters every week asking for help of some sort. Make it easy for them to read your letter and you're more likely to get a response.

2. Be direct

Don't write vague stuff like: 'I'm writing to ask if you might possibly be able to help out with a project I am working on' – this tells nobody anything.

Influential voices

3. Get to the point – fast!

20 For example: 'Young people in this area are about to lose their only local theatre club. I'm campaigning to stop that happening.'

4. Explain who you are

25 How are you connected with the issue? Why do you feel so strongly about it?

For example: 'I'm a member of a youth drama club with 85 members from this town all aged between 13 and 18. We put on five plays each year, and it's a real
30 chance for us to meet up and do something fun.'

5. Give the facts

● What is the campaign about?

● Who does it affect?

35 ● How will it improve things?

● What are you doing to make it happen?

For example: 'The youth theatre is closing because the council can't afford to mend the roof and make it safe. There is no other
40 theatre within walking distance where we can all meet, so the youth drama club will have to close too. We want to raise £8,000 to pay for the work and keep the theatre open.'

What Michelle did

Michelle sent a letter to her local MP complaining about the state of the area she lives in, which she says doesn't have its own hospital, cinema or any decent places to go.

'I showed the letter I was going to send to my mum. She checked it out for me because I'm terrible at spelling. She said it was fine but that I was a bit abrupt. So I made it a bit tamer. If I received a letter and it was really rude, I know I wouldn't do anything about it.'

'My dad's reaction was like, "If you think you're going to get somewhere with this, you've got another think coming." When I got a letter back replying to mine, he was like, "Oh my God!" He was so surprised.'

Key Reading

Advice texts

This is an **advice** text. Its **purpose** is to give advice and persuade the reader to take it.

The main features of this text are:

● It presents a **series of points**, often made easy to read by **presentational devices**. For example, the main points have numbered headings.

● It provides **examples** of how to write the letter, for example, 'I am a member of a youth drama club…

● It uses **direct address** to speak to the reader, for example, '*Try* to write no more than 300 words.'

● It uses a **conversational, informal tone** to get on the reader's side, for example, '*Don't* write vague *stuff* like…'

1 Apart from the numbered headings, what other **presentational devices** are used on this webpage?

2 Find one example offered of **how to write**, and one example of **how not to write** a letter to a celebrity.

3 How does the writer **address the reader** in this extract?

4 Find two examples of the writer's **conversational tone** in points 1 and 2. Explain why this tone has been used.

Purpose

5 The purpose of the webpage is stated in its title. But what is the exact purpose of:

   a) the **first eight lines** (before the numbered points begin)?

   b) the **side panel** 'What Michelle did'?

Reading for meaning

6 The text begins with the two sentences, 'Politicians and celebs. Love them or hate them, they're hard to ignore.' (lines 1–2)

   a) What is special about the **first sentence**?

   b) What **effect** do these sentences have at this point in the text?

7 Look at the numbered headings. How have the **writer** and the **designer** tried to make them as clear as possible? Have each of them succeeded?

8 Michelle's quote is even more informal than the rest of the writing on the webpage.

   a) Give an example of **colloquial language** used by Michelle.

   > **colloquial** refers to the language used in conversation

   b) Rewrite your example in **formal language**.

9 How good are the writer's **examples** of how to write? Analyse the example about the youth theatre in point 5 by comparing it against the bullet-point list of what facts to include.

Focus on: Presentational devices

How you present your advice visually is also important. For example, using too many different fonts is confusing for the eye, and distracts the reader from the advice itself.

10 In small groups, discuss the **visual presentation** of the webpage. Draw up an evaluation table like the one below. Be prepared to present this to the class.

Presentational device	Good points	How to improve
font(s) used	same font used – very clear	could have different font in the 'Michelle' sidebar for variety
use of colour		
use of bullet points and headings		
overall design		
photo used		

11 Imagine that you were designing a **leaflet** rather than a webpage for this advice. Would you change any of these features? If so, how?

Key Writing

12 **Write the next section of the webpage**, which advises readers on how to check their campaign letter.

a) First, **brainstorm** what you want to say. Jot your main points down the left-hand side of the paper. Add any supporting points or good words/phrases on the right, like this:

type the letter on a computer

better than scribbling it in poor handwriting

save it before you print it

good presentation is half the battle

You may want to cover some or all of these points:
- checking spelling/grammar
- checking that your main points are clear
- including name, address and contact numbers
- layout/presentation of letter
- keeping it brief.

b) Now arrange your points in a **logical order**. This forms the plan for your section.

c) Use your plan to **draft the section**. Remind yourself of the key features of advice texts before you start – for example, using direct address and a conversational tone.

Here are some possible sentence starters:

'Why don't you...?'   'It's no good scribbling...'
'Check how many words...'   'Have you included...?'
'Good grammar makes a difference, because...'

d) Finally, **write up** your section and check it. Add a heading and effective presentational devices.

④ Unit 3 Assignment: Mobiles for mums

Assessment Focus

▶ AF2 Produce texts appropriate to task, reader and purpose

You: work in the advertising department of a mobile phone company.

Your task: to write a leaflet persuading older people to buy your range of mobile phones. You will need your skills in persuasive writing.

· ·

Stage 1

In pairs, **discuss what form** the leaflet will take:

● How much of it will be text, and how much image?

● What images do you want to include, and why?

● What will be the overall tone of the leaflet? (Think about the audience.)

Stage 2

Now **brainstorm some ideas** for the text. Think how you could persuade older people that mobile phones are a good idea.

Jot down your main points on the left-hand side of a piece of paper. Add supporting points or good words/phrases on the right, like this:

| useful for emergencies when travelling | you may need to call the AA/emergency services |
| | tell your loved one you'll be late |

Think about including some of these points:
- where/when a mobile is useful
- how easy it is to use
- how the expense can be kept down.

Tick the best three points from your brainstorm and list them in the most effective order. Add further key phrases or supporting points if they are missing.

Stage 3

Now **write your leaflet**. Remember:

- Use **emotive language**, for example:
'Waiting at the roadside? Worried about a loved one?'

- Begin each paragraph with a sentence that makes the **main point** clear.

- Use **direct address** to grab the reader and to get them on your side.

- Include some **rhetorical devices** such as repetition, sound effects or making a list.

Then add the final touches:

- Think of an attention-grabbing **title**.

- Give your paragraphs snappy **headings**.

Challenge

Think of a name for your phone company, and a good slogan and add these to your leaflet.

Inside poetry

① On the eighth day…

Aims

▶ Read the poem *On the eighth day…*
▶ Learn what parody means (S7)
▶ Identify the language used and the form of a poem
▶ Use the poem as a model to write your own (Wr8)

Read the following poem by Claire Calman. What does it remind you of?

On the eighth day…

In the beginning God created the heaven and the
    earth…
…and the computer.
And God said, Let there be light.
5 And the computer said: Sorry, a system error has
    occurred.
And God said, This is not what I had planned for the
    first day.
On the second day,
10 God said, let there be hardware and let there be
    software and let there be specialists, each who may
    comprehendeth one yet not the other.
And the computer said: This disk is incompatible.
On the third day,
15 God said, let there be disks of many diverse kinds, each
    yielding forth its own programme and let each

become redundant even on the same day it finally becomes affordable.

On the fourth day,

20 God said, Good grief, do I really have to wait till Sunday for the rest?

And the computer said: Please check connections and try again.

And God spent the fifth day listening to Richard

25 Clayderman music while on hold for technical support.

On the sixth day,

God saw that there was not a man to till the ground and He said,

30 Let there be man to have dominion over the sea and the earth and – with any luck – over this computer.

And the Lord God breathed life

Into the microchips that lay scattered on the earth and, lo, there was…

35 Bill Gates.

On the seventh day,

God said, I really could do with a small nap.

On the eighth day,

The computer unplugged God and deleted Him from

40 the system software.

Richard Clayderman a popular pianist

Key Reading

Poetry

This text is a **poem**. Its **purpose** is to explore feelings and ideas.

A poem is made up of **images**, **rhythm** and **form**.

- The **images** are the pictures made by the words.
- The **rhythm** is like the beat in music.
- The **form** is the framework or pattern of the poem. This can vary greatly.

A poem can be written:

- in any number of lines
- in a set number of lines that follow certain rules (for example, a sonnet)
- in verses
- as a word picture (for example, a shape poem).

Poems can be written in different styles:

- Some poems **rhyme**.
- Some poems are **free verse**. They have lines of different lengths with different rhythms. (Some free verse contains rhyme.)

1 **a)** What is the poem **about**?

    b) What happens **at the end**?

2 Which of the following **features** fit this poem?

> free verse   written in verses   regular rhythm
> rhymes   repeating pattern   lines of different lengths
> lines of the same length

Purpose

3 Why might the poet have written the poem? **Add two more reasons** to the following:

- she wanted to have some fun with words
- she was annoyed with her computer
- she had a good idea for the form of the poem.

Reading for meaning

The poem is a **parody**, a type of comic poem in which the poet mimics the style of another writer or poem. This creates a comic effect, but the original must be a serious piece of writing for parody to work.

S7

4 What is the poet **mimicking** in this poem?

5 Where does the **original** come from?

Read the opening lines of the poem and the notes below:

In the beginning God created the heaven and the earth...
...and the computer.

For parody to work the reader must be able to recognise where these lines come from or the style used

Adding this surprise creates humour

Archaic language

Archaic language refers to old-fashioned words and phrases that are no longer in use. As you may have guessed, the poem is written in the style of the Creation story from the *Book of Genesis* in the Bible. The writer uses several techniques to create humour.

- Archaic words and expressions are used. For example, 'Let there be…' (Today we would say 'There will be…'.)

- A mock archaic style is used. Modern vocabulary is used alongside old-fashioned expressions, for example, 'Let there be specialists, each who may comprehendeth…'

6 In pairs, read through the poem and find **two more examples** of each of these techniques.

. . . .

Focus on: The conversation poem

This poem is also a conversation between God and the computer.

7 Discuss the following with a partner:

a) What is the **relationship** like between the two?

b) Who **speaks** most often?

8 Work in groups of three to **read the poem aloud**. Decide on the best way to divide up the lines between the group. To help you do this, consider:

- exactly who is speaking, and when
- where there is a commentary or narrator's voice.

As you read the poem, pay attention to the different styles used and the tones of voice. For example, how is the computer's 'voice' different to God's? Identify the words and expressions that show this contrast.

Repetition

Once you have read the poem aloud, you should be more aware of the repeating pattern in the poem. This gives the poem form.

9 **a)** Look through the poem again and find the **repeating pattern**.

  b) Where is there a major **change** in the pattern? Why?

10 Now read the following. It is the first few lines of a poem by Christopher Smart (1722–1771) written in praise of his cat, in eighteenth century English. **Read the notes** accompanying it.

Of Jeoffrey, His Cat

For I will consider my Cat Jeoffrey.
For he is the servant of the living God, duly and daily serving him.
For at the First glance of the glory of God in the East he worships
  in his way.
5 *For is this done by wreathing his body seven times round with*
  elegant quickness.
For then he leaps up to catch the musk, which is the blessing of
  God upon his prayer.
For he rolls upon prank to work it in.
10 *For having done duty and received blessing he begins to consider*
  himself.
For this he performs in ten degrees.
For first he looks upon his fore-paws to see if they are clean.
For secondly….

Capital letters are used more freely

Repetition and listing gives the poem form and helps to create rhythm

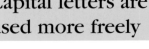

Key Writing

Wr8 **11** Your task is to **write a poem** complaining about or praising the latest IT device that interests you. For example, it might be the latest sound system, mobile phone or PC.

a) First **choose a repeating pattern** for your poem.

- If you write in complaint, you could refer to *On the eighth day…* and start:

  'In the beginning God created heaven and earth…and… (add your IT device)

  On the first day…

  On the second day…'

- If you write in praise, you could start in the same way as *Of Jeoffrey, His Cat*:

  'For I will consider my…' (add your IT device)

b) Once you have decided on your pattern, **note down your main ideas**. Try to use a mix of archaic and everyday language. Use your notes to **produce a first draft**.

c) Ask a partner to **read your draft** and find up to three ways it might be improved. Could the style of the voices contrast more? Could the archaic language sound more authentic? Does the humour in the complaint come through?

d) **Redraft your poem** on a computer, using your partner's suggestions. Choose fonts to suit the style of your poem, including one to suit the archaic language you have used.

② Two views on love

Aims

▶ Read two poems by different poets from different times

▶ Identify the themes of both poems

▶ Look closely at the texts

▶ Consider the form of each poem

▶ Compare the two poems (R17, Wr17)

This poem is by Lord Byron (1788–1824). He belonged to a group of poets called the Romantics. They were interested in emotions, the imagination, nature and freedom of expression.

When we two parted

When we two parted
In silence and tears,
Half-broken hearted,
To sever for years,
5   Pale grew thy cheek and cold,
Colder thy kiss,
Truly that hour foretold
Sorrow to this!

The dew of the morning
10   Sunk chill on my brow;
It felt like the warning
Of what I feel now.
Thy vows are all broken,
And light is thy fame:
15   I hear thy name spoken
And share in its shame.

They name thee before me,
A knell to mine ear;
A shudder comes oe'r me –
20 Why wert thou so dear?
They know not I knew thee
Who knew thee too well:
Long, long shall I rue thee
To deeply to tell.

25 In secret we met:
In silence I grieve
That thy heart could forget,
Thy spirit deceive.
If I should meet thee
30 After long years,
How should I greet thee? –
With silence and tears.

knell a solemn bell; often
  rung at funerals
oe'r over
wert were
rue regret

This poem by John Agard takes a different view of love, perhaps a wiser one.

Anancy's Thoughts on Love

(Anancy is a trickster spider-man figure traditional to Caribbean folk tales)

Love got teeth
as old people say
don't know if you walking
on your hand or your feet
5 but it don't really matter
cause you bound to meet
sooner or later

love is watching hint
big and bold
10 but refusing to catch it

love is trapping thoughts
in side-eye gaze
long before thoughts see light-of-day

love is sweet mystery
15 like sleight-of-rain

but love is sweet misery
like taste-of-pain

love is going down winding labyrinth
at loss for words
20 and loss of head

but Anancy thank God
always have piece of thread
for way back out

or to put it another way
25 Anancy in love
always save back piece of heart
for peace of mind

Key Reading

Poetry

These texts are **poems**. Their **purpose** is to explore feelings and ideas.

A poem is made up of **images**, **rhythm** and **form**.

- The **images** are the pictures made by the words.
- The **rhythm** is like the beat in music.
- The **form** is the framework or pattern of the poem. This can vary greatly.

A poem can be written:

- in any number of lines
- in a set number of lines that follow certain rules (for example, a sonnet)
- in verses
- as a word picture (for example, a shape poem).

Poems can be written in different styles:

- Some poems **rhyme**. Poems with regular rhyming patterns are said to have a **rhyme scheme**.
- Some poems are **free verse**. They have lines of different lengths with different rhythms. (Some free verse contains rhyme.)

1 a) How do you think the **speaker** in *When we two parted* **feels**? Do you agree with any of the ideas below? You can choose more than one.

fearful	angry	resigned	rejected	hurt	betrayed
wistful	surprised	silenced	accepting	bitter	

b) Find words in the poem as **evidence** for your choices. For example, you could say that 'it felt like the warning' in verse 2 suggests the speaker is fearful.

2 Look at the **form** of both poems. How are they differently laid out?

3 How does the **speaker feel** at the end of *Anancy's Thoughts on Love*?

Purpose

4 What do you think Byron's **main purpose** was when he wrote *When we two parted*? To help you, refer to the information about the Romantics above the poem.

5 a) What do you think **Anancy** would think of the feelings expressed in Byron's poem?

b) Is *When we two parted* **relevant** to young people today? Why or why not? Think of more than one reason.

Reading for meaning

Byron's poem explores the emotions felt when a love affair is over. The **mood** is intense and dramatic. Repetition and alliteration (the repetition of the sounds at the beginning of words) are used for effect.

> Pale grew thy cheek and cold,
> Colder thy kiss,
> Truly that hour foretold
> Sorrow to this!

the hard 'c' emphasises a hard heart

the past haunts the present

intense feeling expressed

There are also mysteries and warnings in Byron's poem. The lover's name is never mentioned, and there is the suggestion of a secret.

6 In pairs, discuss what the following lines **suggest**. Think of more than one idea for each. Find the lines in their verses first and look for clues.

> **a)** I hear thy name spoken
> And share in its shame.
>
> **b)** They name thee before me,
> A knell to mine ear;
>
> **c)** In secret we met:
> In silence I grieve
> That thy heart could forget,
> Thy spirit deceive.

The stanza

A **stanza** is another name for a verse. When we use the term 'stanza' we are referring to a poem that has regular patterns. For example, a poem written in stanzas often has:

- the same number of lines in each verse
- the same pattern of rhyme or **rhyme scheme**.

7 a) Look again at *When we two parted*. **How many lines** are there in each stanza?

b) What is the **rhyme scheme** in the first verse? Continue the model below.

| 'When we two parted | a |
| In silence and tears,' | b |

c) Is this pattern **the same** throughout the poem or not?

The patterns in the poem may be regular and ordered but, in contrast, the feelings involved are anything but ordered and controlled. By creating a regular pattern the poet is trying to order and understand this mixture of feelings.

Focus on: Another point of view

In *Anancy's Thoughts on Love*, the poet uses a figure from Caribbean folk tales to explore love in a different way. Anancy has a cooler, more cautious attitude to love.

8 **a)** What does the word '**trapping**' suggest about love in these lines?

> love is trapping thoughts
> in side-eye gaze

b) **What is Anancy**? What does love in the poem have in common with him? Refer back to the lines above.

c) 'Love got teeth' (line 1). **Find other lines** in the poem that show love in this way.

9 **a)** What **advice** would Anancy give about love? Reread the last two verses.

b) Anancy's advice could be **viewed as**:

> **A** selfish   uncaring   lacking commitment

> **B** realistic   wise   canny

 In pairs, **discuss** which view you would **agree with** and why.

Rhythm

Anancy's Thoughts on Love is written in free verse. Remember that although free verse does not have a regular rhythm, it still has rhythm.

10 In pairs, try reading the poem aloud and note down lines that sound particularly **rhythmic**.

Another feature that enhances rhythm is the use of compound words, for example, 'sleight-of-rain'. Not only do the words create vivid images, but they run together, bringing a new rhythm.

11 Find some other examples of **compound words** in the poem.

12 Free verse may contain rhyme, though we do not always notice it at first. Read the poem again together. Discuss how the rhymes **help the rhythm** along.

Key Writing

R17, Wr17

13 **a)** Work with a partner to **compare the two poems** about love. First, draw up a table like the one below and use it to record the similarities between the poems. There are fewer of these than differences, so you will need to search carefully for them. Add lines from each poem as evidence to support your ideas, as shown in this example:

When we two parted / Anancy's Thoughts on Love		
Similarities	Evidence: *When we two parted*	Evidence: *Anancy's Thoughts on Love*
Both poems acknowledge love can be painful	'When we two parted In silence and tears'	'but love is sweet misery like taste-of-pain'

b) Now add the heading '**Differences**' and continue the table, focusing on the differences between the two poems.

Keep your work for the end assignment (pages 93–95).

③ A strange welcome

- Read two poems by the same poet
- Identify the themes of the poems
- Consider the issues in the poems (R16)
- Compare the two poems (Wr17)

The following two poems are from the same volume of poetry, *Propa Propaganda*, by Benjamin Zephaniah. As you read them, think about the connections between the two poems, as well as the poet's concerns.

Homeward Bound

That old man
Cut sugarcane in Jamaica
After he graduated from Sunday School,
Fed up with cutting cane
5   He came here for a better life.
He came here on a big ship
With big dreams
And two guineas,
He came here full of hope
10   With a great big smile,
He came here for the welcome
And the promise.
If his mother (bless her soul) could see him now
She would cry for her baby.

15   He don't understand political correctness
Give him the money and he's gone,
He did not study the oral tradition
Give him a stage and
He will explain.
20   He came here with his ambitions
And his Christianity,

She came here with a nursery qualification
And his Christianity,
Between them they produced six Rastafarians
25   Who called themselves Lost Africans.

When the old man puts on his old suit
He dances like a rude boy
His music is in his head,
Now he dreams of fresh sugar cane,
30   When the old man
Puts on his everyday face
He is only grinning and bearing,
He did forty years on the buses
And he never went to jail.

35   The old man
Was going home anyway,
All his Jamaica nights are in his head,
Fed up with the weather
He wants a better life,
40   All his English days he voted Labour
But he thinks that Labour didn't vote for him,
And now he only wants to see his saviour
Sweet Jamaica.

That old man
45   Shall die in Kensal Rise
He knows it,
You know it
But don't tell him.

Neighbours

I am a type you are supposed to fear
Black and foreign
Big and dreadlocks
An uneducated grass eater.

5   I talk in tongues
I chant at night
I appear anywhere,
I sleep with lions
And when the moon gets me
10 I am a Wailer.

I am moving in
Next door to you
So you can get to know me,
You will see my shadow
15 In the bathroom window,
My aromas will occupy
Your space,
Our ball will be in your court.
How will you feel?

20 You should feel good.
You have been chosen.

I am the type you are supposed to love
Dark and mysterious
Tall and natural

25 Thinking, tea total.
I talk in schools
I sing on TV
I am in the papers,
I keep cool cats

30 And when the sun is shining
I go Carnival.

Benjamin Zephaniah

87

Key Reading

Poetry

These texts are **poems**. Their **purpose** is to explore feelings and ideas.

A poem is made up of **images**, **rhythm** and **form**.

- The **images** are the pictures made by the words.
- The **rhythm** is like the beat in music.
- The **form** is the framework or pattern of the poem. This can vary greatly.

A poem can be written:

- in any number of lines
- in a set number of lines that follow certain rules (for example, a sonnet)
- in verses
- as a word picture (for example, a shape poem).

Poems can be written in different styles:

- Some poems **rhyme**. Poems with regular rhyming patterns are said to have a **rhyme scheme**.
- Some poems are **free verse**. They have lines of different lengths with different rhythms. (Some free verse contains rhyme.)

1 In *Homeward Bound*, **where** does the old man live, and where does he want to be? How do you know?

2 The poem contains many vivid images of the old man. For example: 'When the old man puts on his old suit/He dances like a rude boy (lines 26–27).'

What is the most **striking image** of the Rastafarian in *Neighbours*?

3 What **image** came into your mind as you finished *Homeward Bound*?

Purpose

4 In *Homeward Bound*, the poet explores feelings and ideas through the experiences of the old man. In pairs, discuss **why** Zephaniah wrote *Homeward Bound*. Think of more than one reason.

5 **a)** How does Zephaniah **present** the Rastafarian in *Neighbours*? Look carefully. Is he being entirely serious?

b) **Why** do you think he decided to write this poem?

Reading for meaning

Themes

The **theme** of a poem is the main idea or thread running through it. It is the big idea that connects all the images in the poem to give a deeper meaning. For example, the main theme of a poem might be 'love' or 'death' or 'justice'.

In *Homeward Bound*, the old man is central to the theme, but it could be based on anyone in his situation.

R3

6 **a)** In pairs, use the headings below to **build up a picture** of the old man.

● Study each verse carefully to find information.

● Discuss your ideas, locating, where you can, how the old man feels about his experiences (as in the example).

● Make your notes.

His work in Jamaica

'That old man/Cut sugarcane...' – Fed up with cutting cane; the man is

bored by his work.

His early hopes

His beliefs

His family and work in Britain

His dreams

b) Now discuss how the old man **feels** as his life draws to a close. Focus on the following words, deciding which are useful.

> sad   angry   disappointed   resigned
> broken-hearted   bewildered   satisfied
> regretful   a stranger

c) Finally, decide together on the **main theme** of *Homeward Bound.*

Focus on: Using humour to make a point

In contrast to *Homeward Bound*, *Neighbours* is a serious poem told in a humorous way. In other words, it makes its point by using humour. The poem focuses on a Rastafarian and the kind of prejudice he comes across. He is presented in one way in the first part, and in another in the second. Both views of him are deliberate **stereotypes**.

R16

7 **a)** In pairs, reread verses 1, 2 and 3, and **make notes** under the heading 'Stereotype 1'. Then read verses 4, 5 and 6 and make notes under the heading 'Stereotype 2'.

b) Look carefully for words that give clues as to which **stereotype** is being presented. Add these to your notes. For example, Zephaniah uses a **pun** in the following lines:

'And when the moon gets me
I am a Wailer.' (lines 9–10)

'Wailer' refers to Bob Marley's reggae band 'The Wailers'. What else does it imply?

c) As you work on the poem together, think about when the poet is being **humorous** and when he is being **serious**.

d) Using your notes, decide together what the **main theme** of the poem is.

> **pun** a word with a double meaning, used to make a joke
> **stereotype** an over-simplified, fixed view of someone or something, usually based on prejudice.

Key Writing

Wr17

8 a) In pairs, compare *Homeward Bound* and *Neighbours*. **Draw up a table** like the one below, identifying the **similarities** first. Record **evidence** from each poem to support each similarity.

Homeward Bound/Neighbours		
Similarities	Evidence: *Homeward Bound*	Evidence: *Neighbours*
Both poems deal with issues about belonging	'All his Jamaica nights are in his head'	'I am a type you are supposed to fear / Black and foreign'

b) Now complete the table, focusing on the **differences** between the two poems.

9 On your own, **write three paragraphs** about the poems, using your notes and referring to this plan.

Paragraph 1 – Compare the similarities between the poems. Use connectives such as 'similarly', 'also' and 'in addition' to link your ideas.
Paragraph 2 – Contrast the differences between the poems. Use connectives such as 'alternatively', 'by contrast'
Paragraph 3 – Sum up the issues you think were uppermost in Zephaniah's mind when he wrote these poems, referring back to your work in questions 4 and 5.

Remember to:

● quote lines from the poems to support main points – taken from your table

● punctuate your quotations correctly. For example, when discussing the old man in *Homeword Bound*, you might say:

He arrived in Britain with 'big dreams', 'two guineas' and 'his Christianity'.

④ Unit 4 Assignment: The critic

 Assessment Focus

▶ AF3   Organise and present whole texts effectively, sequencing and structuring information, ideas and events

---

You: are a poetry critic.

Your task: to write an essay comparing two poems.

You will need the work you did on the poems *When we two parted* by Lord Byron and *Anancy's Thoughts on Love* by John Agard on pages 77–84.

Stage 1

First, you are going to **plan** your essay.

Introduction

Open by stating what you are going to do. Name the poems and who wrote them.

Then make two general statements, briefly stating what the poems have in common and how they differ. (For example, they are both about love, but are written from very different points of view.)

The main section

Now compare the two poems in greater detail.

One way of organising your ideas is to write all your points on poem 1 first. Then move on and write about poem 2, comparing it with poem 1.

Choose:

● which poem to begin with   ● which points to include.

Refer to the table from page 84 and select points from this. Make a note of these on your plan.

Then do the same with poem 2, but also:

● compare its similarities with the first poem

● contrast its differences.

Conclusion

Briefly note how you will sum up the main features of each poem, drawing out the contrasts between the two.

· ·

Stage 2

Think about how to **organise** your discursive essay.

Use paragraphs and connectives:

To write well, you will need to organise your points into several paragraphs and link them effectively.

For example, when writing about the poems, use connectives:

● of comparison ('in the same way', 'similarly', 'also')

● of contrast ('on the one hand', 'on the other hand', 'whereas', 'although').

Use quotations (and use them correctly):

Try to support your comments by quoting from the poem.

Use some of the quotes you collected in question 13, page 84.

For example, you could write:

> Byron writes about lost love. John Agard's poem also acknowledges that 'love is sweet misery/like taste-of-pain'.

single quotation marks

Stage 3

Now **write your draft essay**, referring to your plan and the tips provided above. When you have completed your draft, look through it to see what might be improved.

For example, you could improve your essay by extending your sentences and paragraphs. Add more about the similarities or differences between the poems. For example, you might have written:

> 'In both poems the speaker is aware that love can cause pain.'

This could become:

> 'In both poems the speaker is aware that love can cause pain, but in "Anancy's Thoughts on Love" the last lines suggest that we can protect ourselves by not giving everything in love.'

Write the next sentence, which could begin:

> 'Byron's poem, on the other hand, …'

Redraft your essay to produce a final version.

① Stone Cold

Aims

▶ Read the opening scenes of a playscript about being homeless, and explore their dramatic impact (R14)

▶ Perform one of these scenes, focusing on conveying an effective character (S&L14)

▶ Write a critical evaluation of several performances (S&L15)

The following extract is from the opening to a play by Joe Standerline, based on the novel *Stone Cold* by Robert Swindells.

Scene 1

*The street. A litter bin. A yellow spot comes up on **Link**. He looks bored. His clothes are scruffy and he looks dirty. He takes a good look at the*
5 *audience, then speaks to them.*

LINK Have you ever sat and watched people, really watched them? They're all in their own little world. Now and then they'll let you in, if they're feeling brave or if they think they
10 know you. But the rest of the time you might as well be invisible.

A couple of passers-by walk straight in front of him. One drops a crisp packet at his feet.

See what I mean.

15 ***Link*** *picks up the crisp packet and looks to see if there's anything left inside. There isn't. He moves towards the litter bin. The lights fade.*

Scene 2

Shelter's living room. There is an armchair, small
table, standard lamp and fireplace. A doorway leads
from this room to the bathroom and kitchen. There
is a window with heavy, drawn curtains. A cat lies
quietly in a basket in front of the fireplace.
Above is hung a portrait of an old-looking
soldier. *Shelter* enters with a bowl of tomato soup.

SHELTER *(Thinking out loud)* Haven?...
Home...House...

*He sits down, puts his soup on the table and
picks up a dictaphone and starts to record.*

Day One. Everything is ready. Practice
mission executed successfully. Executed.
*(Sniggers. There's a knock at the
door; **Shelter** ignores it.)* Only
complaint at present time is constant
pestering from man upstairs. Have now
verified code name and will shortly post
mission statement to relevant body.
Operation to be known as...

*He stops the tape for a time to think. He
ignores another knock at the door.*

Hostel?...Shack?...Shed?...

Another knock, he is slightly riled.

Shelter! That's it. *(Recording it.)*
'Operation Shelter!' Perfect. Succinct
yet welcoming.

*Switches the tape off and slurps a mouthful of
soup. There's another knock, the soup drips
from his mouth as he speaks.*

Get. Lost.

*He sits at the table and starts to write.
Lights snap back to the street scene.*

executed (1) carried out, (2) killed
verified confirmed
riled annoyed
succinct short and to the point

Key Reading

Play scripts

This text is a **play script**. The script's **purpose** is to provide a written version of the play for actors, the director and anyone else developing the play.

The main features of this text are:

● Its **layout** includes text divided into scenes and the names of the characters on the left in capitals. The words of the characters follow their names.

● It presents **visual information/directions** in italics. These can describe a scene or a character's actions, for example *'A couple of passers-by walk straight in front of him.'*

● It contains **dialogue/speech** which is not presented in inverted commas, for example: '**SHELTER**   Haven?… Home…House…'

● It contains **monologues**, which let the audience know what is going on in the character's head, for example: '**LINK**   Have you ever sat and watched people, really watched them?'

> **monologue** a speech made directly to the audience which reveals a character's inner thoughts

1 Describe in one or two sentences what happens in Scene 1. Then do the same for Scene 2. Refer to the **character** and **setting** of each scene in your answer.

2 Find one **stage direction** in each scene. How do you know these are stage directions?

3 Both Link and Shelter are alone in their scenes. So **who** are they talking to?

Purpose

4 A play script gives you more information than the actors' lines. What does this extract tell you about the **lighting effects** in these two scenes?

5 Scene 1 is very short, and not much happens. So why did Joe Standerline start his play with it? **Discuss the following opinions** in pairs. Which is closest to your own view? Find evidence in Scene 1 to support your choice.

> He wants to show right at the start what being homeless is really like.

> He wants to make us wonder who this young man is and why he's homeless.

> He wants to grab the audience's attention by getting Link to speak directly to them.

Reading for meaning

6 In what **tone** do you think Link says his words in Scene 1?

● thoughtful   ● angry   ● bored   ● resigned

In pairs, take turns saying the lines in these different ways. Which seems most effective?

7 Much more detail about the setting is given in the stage directions to Scene 2. It is as if the writer wants to contrast the two settings. How could you **bring out this contrast** in an actual production?

8 Someone knocks at Shelter's door throughout Scene 2.

a) How does Shelter **react** to each knock?

b) What effect does the continued knocking have on the **atmosphere** this early in the play?

Focus on: Conveying character

S&L14

9 Your task is to **direct and perform Scene 2**. Shelter must come across as both strange and dangerous. He is described in the cast list as:

'In his early forties; one serious head-case; thrown out of the army for being out of control.'

a) Discuss the following questions in pairs:

● What does Shelter look like? How is he dressed, and how does he walk?

● How does he say his lines? Notice the short sentences (remember, he was in the army).

● Does Shelter appear threatening straight away? Or does this happen gradually through the scene? How could you present this?

Also consider your answer to question 8 in your discussion.

b) Make notes on a copy of Scene 2 to bring out exactly how you would play the scene. For example:

Come in briskly

Slightly irritated at not coming up with right name

> **Shelter** enters with a bowl of tomato soup.
>
> **SHELTER** (Thinking out loud)
>   Haven?...Home...House...
>
> He sits down, puts his soup on the table and picks up a dictaphone and starts to record.

Leave good pauses between words

Don't slump – do everything crisply

c) Still in pairs, one of you takes the role of director and the other the actor playing Shelter. **Rehearse the scene**, making changes to your notes if necessary.

Key Speaking and Listening

10 Now join up with three other pairs. Each pair performs Scene 2. Meanwhile, the other pairs **make notes** on the performance. **Draw up a table** like the one below, and record your thoughts:

	Pair 1	Pair 2	Pair 3	Pair 4
Acting – Does Shelter: ● engage our attention? ● present a convincing character? ● develop through the scene?				
Directing – Is there: ● a sense of purpose and direction to the scene? ● a build-up of tension? ● any unusual interpretation? With what effect?				

Make sure you include an evaluation of your own performance.

interpretation a particular approach to a performance, which makes that performance different from others

Killing with kindness

Aims

▶ Read a poster and webpage produced by a homelessness charity

▶ Explore how a persuasive case is presented

▶ Present a more biased case, and analyse the bias used by others (Wr13, S&L6)

The poster below and webpage on page 103 are both part of a campaign by Thames Reach Bondway, a homelessness charity.

Can you spare 20p for a cup of tea?
How about £10 for a bag of heroin?
Or £12 for a rock of crack?

The money you give to those who beg may help keep them on the streets. It may even help to buy the drugs that kill them. Put your spare change where it counts instead. Thames Reach Bondway – Ending street homelessness.

Killing with Kindness

Why Thames Reach Bondway believe giving to those who beg does more harm than good.

> "Don't be mean, you heard the man, he wants a few pence for a cup of tea..."

The overwhelming evidence shows that people who beg on the street do so in order to buy hard drugs – particularly crack cocaine and heroin. These Class A drugs are highly addictive and eventually lead to extreme deterioration in health and even death.

Drug testing of people arrested for begging in Westminster disclosed that 77% of those arrested tested positive for Class A drugs.

> "Maybe, but there's surely no harm in giving a few pence..."

Giving to people who beg is not a benign act without consequences. As an organisation that has worked with people on the street for over twenty years, we have seen many lives damaged by hard drugs and alcohol misuse. People have also died through overdoses. A significant portion of their income that was spent on drugs came from members of the public giving loose change.

> "OK, you've convinced me. So how can I help people to get off the street and away from the dealers?"

Here are some recommended alternatives to handing out 'spare change':
- You can buy the person a cup of tea or sandwich instead.
- You can spend time listening to them and finding out more about their needs.
- You can donate to a charity working with homeless people who can guarantee (and if necessary provide evidence) that your money is going directly to homeless people. Thames Reach Bondway is able to do so.
- You can volunteer to work with a homelessness agency such as Thames Reach Bondway. To find out more, contact Tara Butler on 020 7702 5647 or via our website, www.thamesreachbondway.com.

Help Thames Reach Bondway to end street homelessness.

benign safe, kind

Key Reading

Persuasion texts

These persuasion texts are part of a series of **campaign material**. Their **purpose** is to persuade people not to give to beggars.

The main features of the poster are:

● It uses **visual images** to grab the interest of the audience and make an impact, for example, the figure made up of coins.

● It uses **emotive language**, for example, 'It may even help to buy the drugs that kill them…'

The main features of the webpage are:

● It uses **formal language**, for example, 'Here are some recommended alternatives…'

● It includes **evidence or reasons** given for the points made, for example, 'The overwhelming evidence shows that…'

1 What makes the coin figure on the poster such a **powerful image**? What **message** does it send?

2 How does the **text** on the poster draw you in to read further?

3 a) Which parts of the webpage are written in **formal language**? Which are written in **informal language**?

b) Why have two different '**registers**' been used?

4 The main argument in the webpage is that giving to those who beg does more harm than good.
Find one **reason** that backs up this statement.

> **register** the level of formality of a text; for example, the register of a conversation with a friend is different from that of a formal letter

Purpose

5 Is the **purpose** of the poster and the webpage exactly the **same**? Discuss this question in pairs. Find evidence in the texts to support your answers.

Reading for meaning

6 Who is **asking the questions** at the top of the poster? Who is **giving the explanation** underneath?

7 Both pieces of text on the poster use **direct address** – when the reader is addressed as 'you'. Identify **where** this happens and how **effective** it is.

8 What other **image** could you use on a poster for this campaign? Think of an image of your own, and compare it with the coin figure.

9 The webpage uses a '**question and answer**' format.

   a) Why has it been written like this?

   b) How **effective** is it?

10 The **final section** of the webpage is written and organised in a different way from the rest. Explain how, and say what particular purpose this has.

Focus on: Making a persuasive case

The Thames Reach Bondway webpage makes its case by presenting a reasoned argument with a 'passer-by'. These are the methods used:

● formal language

● giving evidence and facts.

11 Identify **two examples** of each of these features in the two sections of text.

The charity could have chosen a more **biased** way of presenting its case. Features of biased texts often include:

- emotive and rhetorical language – for example, 'killer drugs'
- giving opinions rather than facts – for example, 'It is disgraceful that…'
- using the first and second person to get the audience on side – for example, 'You must not give money'
- stereotyping people – for example, presenting all beggars as drug addicts.

> **biased** unfairly presented to favour one point of view over another

A biased version of the first section could look like this:

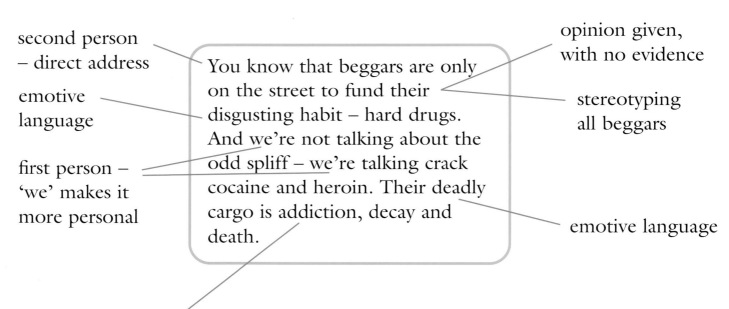

second person – direct address

emotive language

first person – 'we' makes it more personal

> You know that beggars are only on the street to fund their disgusting habit – hard drugs. And we're not talking about the odd spliff – we're talking crack cocaine and heroin. Their deadly cargo is addiction, decay and death.

opinion given, with no evidence

stereotyping all beggars

emotive language

rhetorical effect of list of three, and alliteration of 'd' sound

12 In pairs, **rewrite section 2** of the text in a similar way. Use the techniques listed above to make your text as **biased** as possible.

13 Which is the more **effective** text in your view? Add a comment below your version to explain your answer.

Key Speaking and Listening

14 a) Join up with three other pairs. Then listen carefully as each pair reads out their text from question 12, and note down examples of bias. **Draw up a table** like the one below to record your analysis:

Examples of	Pair 1	Pair 2	Pair 3	Pair 4
emotive and rhetorical language				
opinions rather than facts				
using the first and second person				
stereotypes				

Make sure you include an analysis of your own text.

b) Decide as a group:

● Which is the **most biased** text?

● Which is the **most effective** at biasing the audience?

3 London road

Aims

▶ Read an account of how a famous writer left home

▶ Explore how different tenses are used to describe past events

▶ Use reading and dramatic skills to explore the ideas and meaning of the passage (S&L12)

▶ Write about style, giving evidence from the text (Wr17)

In *As I Walked Out One Midsummer Morning*, Laurie Lee describes how he eventually left his family and home in the Cotswold countryside.

The stooping figure of my mother, waist deep in the grass and caught there like a piece of sheep's wool, was the last I saw of my country home as I left it to discover the world. She stood old and bent at the top of the bank, silently watching
5   me go, one gnarled red hand raised in farewell and blessing, not questioning why I went. At the bend of the road I looked back again and saw the gold light die behind her; then I turned the corner, passed the village school, and closed that part of my life for ever.

10   It was a bright Sunday morning in early June, the right time to be leaving home. My three sisters and a brother had already gone before me; two other brothers had yet to make up their minds. They were still sleeping that morning, but my mother had got up early and cooked me a heavy breakfast,
15   had stood wordlessly while I ate it, her hand on my chair, and had then helped me pack my few belongings. There had been no fuss, no appeals, no attempts at advice or persuasion, only a long and searching look. Then, with my bags on my back, I'd gone out into the early sunshine and climbed through the
20   long wet grass to the road.

It was 1934. I was nineteen years old, still soft at the edges, but with a confident belief in good fortune. I carried a small rolled-up tent, a violin in a blanket, a change of clothes, a tin of treacle biscuits, and some cheese. I was excited, vain-glorious, knowing I had far to go; but not, as yet, how far. As I left home that morning and walked away from the sleeping village, it never occurred to me that others had done this before me.

That first day alone – and now I was really alone at last – steadily declined in excitement and vigour. As I tramped through the dust towards the Wiltshire Downs a growing reluctance weighed me down. White elder-blossom and dog-roses hung in the hedges, blank as unwritten paper, and the hot empty road – there were few motor cars then – reflected Sunday's waste and indifference. High sulky summer sucked me towards it, and I offered no resistance at all. Through the solitary morning and afternoon I found myself longing for some opposition or rescue, for the sound of hurrying footsteps coming after me and family voices calling me back.

None came. I was free. I was affronted by freedom.

gnarled bent, knobbly
vainglorious big-headed
indifference lack of interest
affronted confronted, offended

Key Reading

Recount texts

This text is a **recount**. Its **purpose** is to retell events in an entertaining way.

The main features of this text are:

- It is told mainly in the **past tense**, for example, 'I *turned* the corner.'
- It generally describes events in **time order**.
- It uses **time connectives**, for example, 'Through the solitary morning and afternoon…'
- It uses **descriptive language** to bring the events to life, such as adjectives, powerful verbs and imagery, for example, 'High *sulky* summer *sucked* me towards it.'

1 Find one example of the **simple past** tense and one example of the **past perfect** tense in this text. Try to explain why the tense has been used in each case.

2 At what **time, day, month and year** is the start of this recount set?

3 Find one sentence with **powerful description**. Explain what makes it so **effective**.

Grammar for reading

The most common tense used to refer to a specific event in the past is the **simple past**. The **past perfect** is used to refer to what happened before events described in the past. The form is usually 'had' + past tense: for example 'He *had tidied up* by the time I arrived.'

Purpose

4 This recount text forms part of an autobiography. What is the **purpose** of an autobiography? Is this the main purpose of Laurie Lee's recount?

Reading for meaning

5 Describe how Laurie Lee's **mother** responds to his leaving home. What do you think she is thinking and feeling?

6 How does Laurie Lee himself feel about this day? Chart any **changes in his mood** through the day. Use a table like the one started below:

Time	Mood	Evidence
that morning at breakfast	calm, sure of himself	'the right time to be leaving home'

7 'It never occurred to me that others had done this before me.' (lines 27–28). What does Laurie Lee **mean**?

8 What is the **effect** of the three short sentences that end the extract?
'None came. I was free. I was affronted by freedom.' (line 40)

9 Imagine that you were turning Laurie Lee's book into a stage play. How would you **stage** this opening scene? Think about:
- how you could suggest what has led up to this event
- how you would present Laurie Lee's actual departure
- how you could suggest his change in mood through the day
- what props or scenery and lighting you would use.

S&L12

Focus on: Discussing a writer's style

You may be asked to describe in detail the style of a piece of writing. You should go about doing this in a number of steps.

10 **a)** First, **read** the extract carefully. Look out for the following features:

- **Vocabulary** – Plain or highly descriptive? Any powerful words used? Any sound effects?

- **Imagery** – Any similes, metaphors and personification used?

- **Sentence structure** – Length of sentences? Which are complex or simple? Is there great variety?

b) Look again at paragraph 5 and **make notes** on each of these features, commenting on their effect if you can. For example, you could make notes on the start of paragraph 3 like this:

Short sentence to start paragraph. Contrasts with longer listing sentences and details of his feelings which follow

Metaphor – implies he is like an image in wax – still forming, still 'hardening off', not quite an adult

It was 1934. I was nineteen years old, still soft at the edges, but with a confident belief in good fortune. I carried a small rolled-up tent, a violin in a blanket, a change of clothes, a tin of treacle biscuits, and some cheese. I was excited, vain-glorious, knowing I had far to go; but not, as yet, how far.

The old-fashioned word vain-glorious suggests a knight off on a quest

List of examples show us how little he took with him and gives poignancy to his leaving

One long sentence, carefully controlled; the second half of the sentence is a comment from the adult's point of view

Key Writing

Wr17 **11** Use the question notes you made in question 10 to write at least 100 words analysing the style of paragraph 5. To make your points clearly, you can use the 'Point, Evidence, Comment' technique:

- first state your **point** clearly
- next quote the **evidence** from the text – the key words only, put in inverted commas
- finally, add a **comment** on the effect – saying how well the feature works, or adding a personal comment on its effect.

For example, this is how you could write about Lee's use of imagery:

point – put clearly at the start

evidence – note key words and inverted commas

comment – describes effect of the feature

> Laurie Lee uses a striking metaphor to describe himself as he leaves home. He is a young and inexperienced nineteen-year-old, 'still soft at the edges'. It makes him sound like an image of wax: still impressionable and ready to face new challenges, but also vulnerable.

- Organise your writing in paragraphs – for example, one paragraph on vocabulary.
- Use the correct language for word classes and other terms – for example, adjectives, verbs, similes, metaphors.

113

4 Unit 5 Assignment: Homeless

Assessment Focuses

▶ **AF3** Organise and present whole texts effectively, sequencing and structuring information, ideas and events

▶ **AF4** Construct paragraphs and use cohesion within and between paragraphs

> **You:** are designing a website for a homelessness charity.
>
> **Your task:** to turn some notes from an interview with a homeless person into an effective personal story for the website.

Quotes

"I was too proud to contact my parents."

"That was the worst night of my life. I didn't want to wake up."

"I didn't think I could sink any lower. Begging was so humiliating."

"It was so weird feeling the cool air on my face."

"I've never felt so tired, dirty and hungry."

Key facts

- Name: Terry Davis
- Age: 20
- Present address: Hostel for the homeless, Dudley

Recent history

- June 2004, T. quit job – row with manager. T. couldn't pay rent and bills
- July, left flat, stayed on friends' floors in Dudley, 'overstayed welcome'
- All hostels full – slept in car parks in August
- Befriended by other homeless people
- Had to beg to get food
- Sept – got some benefit money and a room came up in a hostel

Family history

- Grew up in comfortable home in countryside
- Parents divorced when T. was 7
- Mum remarried but T. fell out with stepfather
- At 17 got job in garden centre, moved into flat with girlfriend Sasha.

Stage 1

Read the four pages of notes from the interview with Terry. Discuss with a partner how you will **organise these notes** so that they form the basis of 'Terry's Story'.

Where could you use the quotations? (Try to use at least two of them).

Stage 2

Now **plan your recount**. Organise your notes into what will be three paragraphs. Remember that a new paragraph marks a change of focus in a recount.

In your plan, give your paragraphs the following headings:
- Paragraph 1: A comfortable life
- Paragraph 2: On the street
- Paragraph 3: A roof over our heads.

Stage 3

Now **write your recount**. Remember:
- to put the events in time order
- to use connectives (especially of time) to make the sequence of events clear to the reader
- to include specific names, dates and other details to bring the story alive

● to write in the third person, but add some of Terry's own words for variety and interest. Place inverted commas around the actual words quoted.

main recount written in third person

Three weeks tramping the streets took their toll on Terry and Sasha. "I've never felt so tired, dirty and hungry," Terry said.

quote by Terry in first person; note inverted commas

Challenge

Use ICT to write and design your recount as a webpage. Include:

● a photo of Terry
● an effective heading and subheadings.

① Mother and daughter

Aims

▶ Read a newspaper interview with a mother and daughter

▶ Explore how discursive texts present people's views

▶ Present a balanced report on your friends' views (R2, Wr16)

The following text comes from *The Daily Telegraph*.

Katie believes in God and marriage. Her mother doesn't.

KATIE Lodwidge's life revolves around hair, make-up, shoes and clothes, according to her mother.

The 15-year-old reads teenage magazines, talks for hours to her friends, enjoys dance, singing and aerobics and hates tidying her
5   bedroom.

But behind this façade of normal teenage behaviour, Katie has developed a keen sense of morality and conservative social attitudes which contrast with the more liberal views of her mother, Alyson Pratt, 38.

10   Katie believes strongly in marriage and hopes to walk down the aisle one day. She feels that it is all right for people to have children outside marriage if they love each other and are in a stable relationship, but she wants to get married first.

This surprises Alyson, a legal secretary, who says she did not
15   marry Katie's father. "I don't believe in marriage in this day and age because things have changed and so many marriages end in the heartache and nastiness of divorce."

Katie believes in God. Her mother is an atheist. Katie is proud to be British, her mother is stumped by the question. Katie wants Britain to become more integrated with the rest of Europe, whereas her mother is firmly against it.

At home in Locksheath, near Fareham, in Hampshire, yesterday mother and daughter discovered new things about each other. Katie says abortion is a serious step only to be undertaken when there is a good reason. Alyson supports abortion on demand because it is a woman's right to choose.

On drugs the teenager is against legalisation of cannabis because it will encourage young people to experiment and fail to stop the dealers who will buy up supplies to sell cut-price on the streets. She wants tougher penalties for drugs. Her mother says cannabis should be legalised. "People are going to get hold of it, whether it is against the law or not."

On tougher penalties for crime their views coincide and both would like to see the death penalty brought back for child killers.

Their views diverge again on whether there should be tougher penalties to discourage under-age sex. Katie thinks there should be, to act as a deterrent. Her mother says tougher sanctions would make no difference. "If they want to have sex they will do it and I blame parents. It's up to parents to educate their children about the dangers of under-age sex, not schools. I know of people who allow their 13- and 14-year-old daughters to entertain boyfriends in their bedrooms. That will never happen in this house!"

"I am surprised by some of my daughter's views. I had no idea she was thinking so deeply about the issues," says Alyson. Katie wants to get back to washing her hair.

façade surface layer

conservative traditional, not in favour of rapid change

liberal open-minded, tolerant

integrated connected

diverge differ, disagree

deterrent something that discourages you from acting in a certain way

sanctions punishments

Key Reading

> **Discursive texts**
>
> This is a **discursive** text. Its **purpose** is to present different views as fairly as possible.
>
> The main features of this text are:
>
> - It presents a series of **points** organised into **paragraphs**, for example, the fourth paragraph presents Katie's views on marriage.
>
> - It uses the **present tense**, for example, 'Katie *believes* in God.'
>
> - It presents points supported by **evidence** or **reasons**, for example, 'Alyson supports abortion on demand because it is a woman's right to choose.'
>
> - It uses **formal language**, for example, 'Katie has developed a keen sense of morality.'

1 Find the paragraph on drugs. What are Katie's and Alyson's **views**?

2 "I had no idea she was thinking so deeply about the issues," says Alyson (lines 43 and 44). Why is the **present tense** used for the verb 'says'?

3 'Alyson supports abortion on demand because it is a woman's right to choose' (lines 25 and 26).

    a) Which clause in this sentence gives a **reason** – the first or the second?

    b) Which **connective** signals this to the reader?

4 'Katie says abortion is a serious step only to be undertaken when there is a good reason' (lines 24–25).

    Reword this formal statement using **informal language**.

Purpose

5 What is the **main purpose** of this text?

- To show how teenagers' views are often more traditional than their parents'.
- To argue that teenagers think about issues as deeply as their parents.
- To present the views of a mother and daughter.

Discuss which purpose fits best, finding evidence in the text to support your choice.

Reading for meaning

6 Why is Katie's 'normal teenage behaviour' described as a 'façade' (line 6)?

7 What **issues** are explored in this interview? Draw up a table like the one below, summarising Katie's and her mother's views on each issue.

Issue	Katie	Alyson
marriage	strongly for	against

8 What does the writer mean when she says that Alyson is 'stumped by the question' about being proud to be British (line 19)? What do you think Alyson's answer **actually** was?

9 **Analyse the punctuation** in paragraph 5. Can you identify each punctuation mark, and explain why it has been used?

10 Why does the article end with the words 'Katie wants to get back to washing her hair'? What does this **refer back** to? Is this an **effective ending** in your opinion? Why?

• •

Focus on: Presenting views

There are different ways of contrasting people's views in a discursive text. For example:

Katie believes in God. Her mother is an atheist.

two short sentences, each beginning with the person's name; the contrast in views is **implied**

Katie wants Britain to be more integrated with the rest of Europe, <u>whereas</u> her mother is firmly against it.

here the connective 'whereas' signals the contrast; the contrast is **explicit**

11 **Discuss** these two ways of contrasting Katie and her mother's views. Which is:

a) clearer?

b) more stylish?

Connectives like 'whereas' are very useful in making contrasts clear to the reader. Other connectives that can be used in this way include 'but', 'yet', 'while', 'however', 'on the other hand' and 'in contrast'.

12 In pairs, find a subject that you disagree about. Then **write one sentence** that includes both your views. Rewrite the sentence in **two other ways**, using a different way of signalling the contrast each time.

Points of view can be **quoted directly** or **reported** (see 'Grammar for reading', on page 124). The simplest way of introducing reported speech is to use the reporting verb, 'say':

> 'Katie says abortion is a serious step.'

However, too many 'says' make your writing dull and repetitive. You can vary your approach by:

● using a **different verb** in the reporting clause, for example:

> argue   claim   emphasise   assert
> point out   believe   reply

● **rephrasing the sentence** completely, for example, 'According to her mother…'; 'Katie has a different point to make:…'

13 **Scan** the newspaper article. Note down all the different **reporting verbs** that have been used. What effect does this have?

Grammar for reading

Direct speech is when you quote the exact words that the speaker or writer uses, for example, 'He said, 'We should be allowed to do what we want.'

Reported speech is when the words used are only referred to, or 'reported', for example, 'He said that they should be allowed to do what they wanted.'

no inverted commas are needed

no comma is needed after the reporting clause 'said that…'

the pronoun and the tense of the verb often need changing ('we want' changes to 'they wanted' above)

Key Writing

14 **a)** In groups, **discuss your own views** on these issues:

R2

Wr16

- marriage
- penalties for crime.

Take notes on everyone's views.

b) Then **write up your notes** as a discursive text.

Remember to:

- use connectives if you want to signal contrasting views
- include both direct and reported speech
- vary your reporting verbs
- present everyone's views fairly – including your own.

② Junk the ads?

Aims

▶ Read some emails expressing points of view about fast-food advertising

▶ Make a counter-argument to a view that has been expressed (Wr14)

▶ Compare different points of view (S&L5)

Health and consumer organisations are calling for a ban on junk-food adverts in an attempt to tackle the rise in health-related problems. Here are four email letters written as part of this debate.

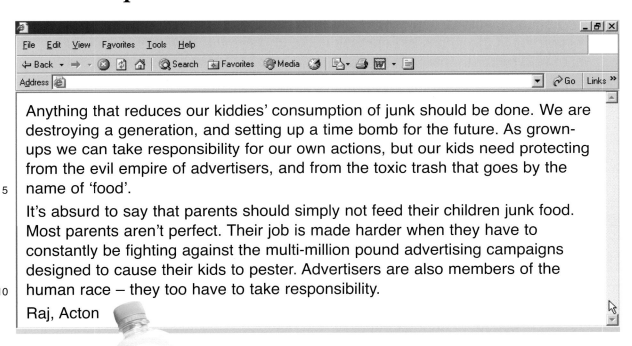

Anything that reduces our kiddies' consumption of junk should be done. We are destroying a generation, and setting up a time bomb for the future. As grown-ups we can take responsibility for our own actions, but our kids need protecting from the evil empire of advertisers, and from the toxic trash that goes by the
5 name of 'food'.

It's absurd to say that parents should simply not feed their children junk food. Most parents aren't perfect. Their job is made harder when they have to constantly be fighting against the multi-million pound advertising campaigns designed to cause their kids to pester. Advertisers are also members of the
10 human race – they too have to take responsibility.

Raj, Acton

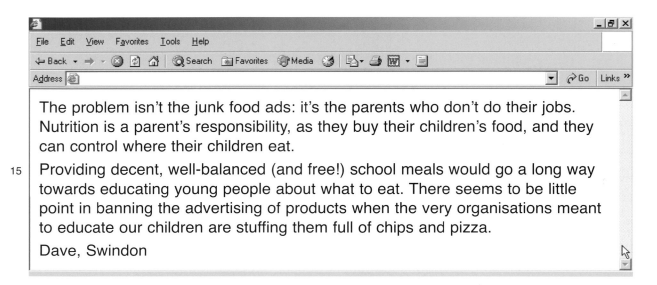

The problem isn't the junk food ads: it's the parents who don't do their jobs. Nutrition is a parent's responsibility, as they buy their children's food, and they can control where their children eat.

15　Providing decent, well-balanced (and free!) school meals would go a long way towards educating young people about what to eat. There seems to be little point in banning the advertising of products when the very organisations meant to educate our children are stuffing them full of chips and pizza.

Dave, Swindon

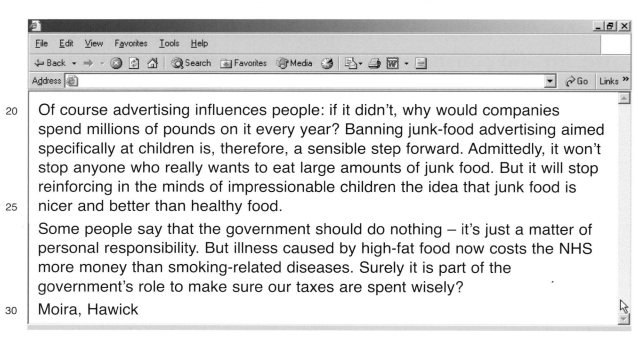

20　Of course advertising influences people: if it didn't, why would companies spend millions of pounds on it every year? Banning junk-food advertising aimed specifically at children is, therefore, a sensible step forward. Admittedly, it won't stop anyone who really wants to eat large amounts of junk food. But it will stop reinforcing in the minds of impressionable children the idea that junk food is
25　nicer and better than healthy food.

Some people say that the government should do nothing – it's just a matter of personal responsibility. But illness caused by high-fat food now costs the NHS more money than smoking-related diseases. Surely it is part of the government's role to make sure our taxes are spent wisely?

30　Moira, Hawick

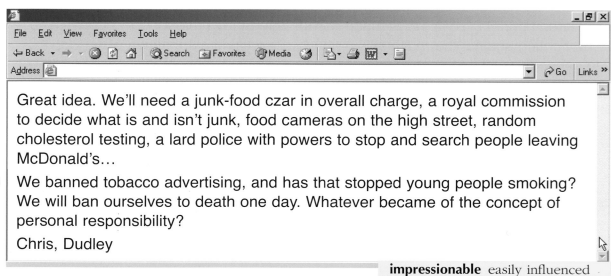

Great idea. We'll need a junk-food czar in overall charge, a royal commission to decide what is and isn't junk, food cameras on the high street, random cholesterol testing, a lard police with powers to stop and search people leaving McDonald's…

35　We banned tobacco advertising, and has that stopped young people smoking? We will ban ourselves to death one day. Whatever became of the concept of personal responsibility?

Chris, Dudley

impressionable easily influenced

czar a Russian emperor, in this context the leader of a public campaign (for example, the 'drugs czar')

Key Reading

Argument texts

These are **argument** texts. Their **purpose** is to argue for a particular point of view.

The main features of these texts are:

● Their **form**, which is a series of **points** backed up by reasons or evidence. For example, Dave's first point is that parents are the problem.

● They use **topic sentences** to introduce each main point, for example, 'Some people say that the government should do nothing.'

● They use a mixture of **formal** and **informal** language, for example, 'The problem isn't the junk-food ads' is written in informal language.

● They use either a **reasonable tone** or **highly emotive tone**, for example, 'the evil empire of advertisers' is an emotive phrase.

1 What **reason** does Dave give for his point that parents, rather than junk-food ads, are the problem?

2 Find two **topic sentences** in Raj and Dave's emails. Explain why these sentences come first in their paragraphs.

3 Identify one sentence written in **formal language**, and one written in **informal language**. Explain what **features** make them formal or informal.

4 a) Which of the emails are written in a **reasonable tone**? Which are written using **emotive language**?

b) In your view, is either approach more **effective** in putting across the argument?

Purpose

5 Which of these texts are arguing **for** a ban on fast-food advertising? Which are arguing **against**?

Reading for meaning

6 Dave offers an **alternative** to banning advertising. What is this alternative?

7 Some of Raj's language is highly **emotive**.

   a) Identify which **words and phrases** are chosen especially to sway the audience's emotions.

   b) Make a comment on the **effect** of each one.

8 Moira makes her argument as **reasonable** as possible. Comment on how the language in each of these sentences represents this reasonable tone:

   a) Banning junk food advertising aimed specifically at children is, therefore, a sensible step forward.

   b) Admittedly, it won't stop anyone who really wants to eat large amounts of junk food.

9 Explain what the **inverted commas** are doing in this phrase from Raj's email:

   ● toxic trash that goes by the name of 'food'.

10 What is **your view** on banning the advertising of junk food? Has your view been altered by the arguments in any of these emails?

Focus on: Counter-arguments

'Attack is the best form of defence.' This idea can apply to argument texts. Sometimes a good way of making your points is to attack, or counter, your opponents' arguments. You can do this in different ways:

> Some people say that the government should do nothing…
> But illness caused by high-fat food now costs the NHS…

the opponent's point is stated, then immediately **countered** by giving a reason why it is wrong

> Great idea. We'll need a junk-food czar in overall charge, a royal commission to decide what is and isn't junk…

the opponent's argument is made to seem **ridiculous**

11 a) Find one way in which the opponent's view is **countered** in Dave's email.

b) Then find one way in which Raj makes the opponent's views seem **ridiculous**.

12 Here are some arguments against a ban on fox hunting. In pairs, put together a **counter-argument** for a ban.

> ● Fox hunting is a traditional country pursuit supported by 60 per cent of people in hunting areas – city-dwellers should not interfere.
>
> ● Fishing is just as cruel as fox hunting – why isn't that criticised?
>
> ● A foxhound kills a fox quickly and cleanly; shooting can cause foxes slow and painful deaths.

a) **Brainstorm** some arguments against fox hunting. Then pick the best two and **write one or two sentences** on each. Remember to use *either* a reasonable tone or an emotive tone, but keep it consistent.

b) Now write one or two sentences **countering** one of the opponent's arguments (above). Are you going to counter this point directly, or make the opponents seem ridiculous for holding this view?

You may like to use one of these phrases:

> **Good phrases to counter an argument:**
>
> The argument that...simply doesn't work.
>
> It isn't the case that...
>
> The main point is not..., but...

> **Good phrases to make the opponent seem ridiculous:**
>
> These absurd people say that...
>
> People must be crazy if they think that...
>
> What sane person would...?

Key Speaking and Listening

S&L5 **13** **a)** Three students are going to read out their arguments against fox hunting. Your job is to listen to the arguments carefully and **compare** them. Jot down some **notes** as you listen.

b) Then organise your notes in a **table**, like the one below:

	Student 1	Student 2	Student 3
What main arguments are used?			
How do they counter the opposing argument?			
Is the tone reasonable or emotive?			
Comment on the overall effectiveness of the argument			

c) Be ready to share your views and to use a **reasonable tone** to express your argument.

131

③ How to party

- ▶ Read an article about coping with parties
- ▶ Understand the impact that complex sentences can make on your writing (S1)
- ▶ Write a piece of humorous advice in an impersonal style (Wr15)

This text comes from a supplement in *The Guardian*.

How to...go to a party

Parties peak between the ages of two and seven, where the high point is cake. There is another peak between 17 and 22, where the high point is the snog. The final peak is between 60 and 75, when cake makes a comeback. After that, the men start dying and the fun goes out of it.

5 There is no greater challenge in modern life than entering a party where you know nobody and everyone is locked into hugely enjoyable conversations with people they love enormously. You have three options at this point. The first and best one is to go home immediately and watch television. However, you will then be tortured by the thought 10 that this was actually the party of a lifetime, where you were on the cusp of meeting the person of your dreams and drinking champagne with them until dawn (someone else can drink the plastic bottle of cider you brought with you).

The next option is to step confidently into the room and say "Excuse 15 me" as you push past various groups as if you were just feet away from joining the group that's waiting so expectantly for you. Keep saying "Excuse me" until you reach a wall and then turn around and make your way back. Do this until you meet someone else doing it or it's time to go home.

20 Option three is to hack your way across the room to the table on which the nibbles are placed. You then have to pretend to be enormously hungry and start eating chopped carrots. If there is nobody at the party you know, you will then eat more carrots than you have eaten up to that point in your adult life. If it's a bowl of cheesy Wotsits, remember

25 that you're likely to be covered head to foot in orange powder by the time you finish.

The nibbles table is the service station for party conversations, so it's often a good place to start conversations with people who are desperate to escape the conversation they've just come from. One good opening

30 line is, "Do you know, from the other side of the room, I thought these carrots were cheesy Wotsits." This also serves as a good closing line.

There are only three cool ways of leaving a party: you can leave it propped up by your mates; you can leave it with someone gorgeous on your arm; or you can pretend you're going on to a cool club. Remember,

35 it's very difficult to pretend that you're going on somewhere exciting if you're sober, by yourself and covered in Wotsits dust.

on the cusp of at the point of

Key Reading

Advice texts

This is an **advice** text. Its **purpose** is to persuade you to do something in a particular way.

The main features of this text are:

- Its **form**, which is a series of **points** in a logical order, for example, the first point made is about the **ages** when parties are most important.

- It uses **direct address** to the reader, for example, '*You* have three options at this point.'

- It uses **causal connectives** to show the consequences of actions, for example, '*If* it's a bowl of cheesy Wotsits, remember…'

- It uses an **impersonal tone** to suggest authority, for example, 'There are only three cool ways of leaving a party'.

1 What is the **second main point** that the author makes?

2 Find three examples of **direct address** in the article.

3 Look at the last sentence of the article. Identify the **cause**, the **consequence**, and the **causal connective** that signals to the reader that this is a causal sentence.

4 Find one other place in the article where the author's tone takes on an air of **authority**.

Purpose

5 This article is written as a self-help advice text. But what is its **main purpose**? Find evidence in the text for your answer.

Reading for meaning

6 A good way of summarising the content of an advice text is to use a **text skeleton**. The main points go on the left, and supporting points or further detail on the right. The skeleton for the article has been started for you below. Write it out and complete it to give a full set of notes on the article.

> 1. The ages when parties are important
> — age 2–7, high point = cake
> — age 17–22, high point = snog
> — age 60–75, high point = cake
> — after that, no fun

7 One technique the writer uses is giving each paragraph a powerful ending, or '**punchline**'. Choose two paragraphs and explain why the writer has ended them the way he has.

8 The author uses imagery in a colourful way in this article. In line 20 he suggests that you 'hack your way' across the room.

   a) What **image** does this suggest?

   b) How **effective** is it?

9 Cheesy Wotsits become a **motif** in this article. Why do you think the author keeps returning to them? Is it successful?

> **motif** a theme or idea that is revisited in a piece of writing or music

Focus on: Using complex sentences

'The nibbles table is the service station for party conversations.'
'It's often a good place to talk to people.'

The connection between the ideas in these two **simple sentences** is not made clear.

You could join the two sentences with 'and' to make a **compound** sentence, but the connection of ideas is still unclear:

'The nibbles table is the service station for party conversations and it's often a good place to talk to people.'

Using a **complex** sentence, however, links the ideas effectively:

'The nibbles table is the service station for party conversations, *so* it's often a good place to talk to people.'

Note the connective 'so', which comes before the subordinate clause. It shows the link with the main clause.

10 Choose a **different connective** for the sentence above but still keep the same meaning.

> **Grammar for reading**
>
> A **complex** sentence usually includes a main clause and a subordinate clause. The main clause can make sense on its own. The subordinate clause begins with a connective – for example, 'when', 'before', 'after', 'since', 'where', 'because', 'although', 'if' or 'until'.

S1 **11** Think up **three complex sentences** based on the two simple sentences below. Be prepared to explain why your sentences bring out the meaning better than the original.

● Mike and Anna turned up at the party.
● I decided to leave.

Key Writing

12 **Write a humorous piece** in the style of the party article called 'How to…dance'. It should be only two paragraphs long.

a) Discuss with a partner some advice points that you could give about dancing. (You will need to decide whether you are advising adults or young people.) Jot these down.

b) Draw up a text skeleton like the one you created to analyse the structure of 'How to…go to a party' in question 6. Write the two best points on the left, and list some supporting points or details on the right.

c) As you draft your article, think about the following:

● Is your tone impersonal, to suggest an air of authority, or is it more informal?

● Do both paragraphs begin with a clear topic sentence?

● Do both paragraphs end with a punchline?

● Can you use complex sentences to make the connection between your ideas clear?

You may like to begin like this:

The people who look the most ridiculous on the dance floor…

④ Unit 6 Assignment: The future is bright

🖉 Assessment Focus

▶ **AF3** Organise and present whole texts effectively, sequencing and structuring information, ideas and events

> **You:** are writing a letter to a newspaper. The newspaper ran an article arguing that technology will make our lives miserable within twenty years.
>
> **Your task:** to argue that technology will make our lives better.

Stage 1

Think of all the ways in which technology may make our lives better over the next twenty years. **Draw up a spidergram** to list your key points. For example:

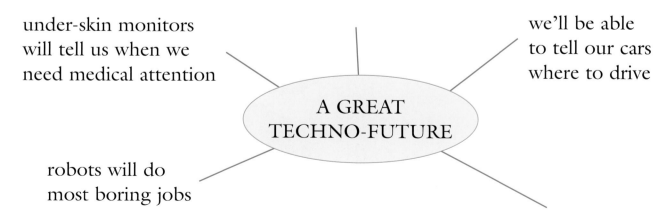

under-skin monitors will tell us when we need medical attention

we'll be able to tell our cars where to drive

A GREAT TECHNO-FUTURE

robots will do most boring jobs

Stage 2

Now **plan your letter**. Choose your three best points that argue for the benefits of technology in the future. Write down a brief summary of each one.

You are going to write a short paragraph on each main point.
- Begin with a general statement explaining why you are writing.
- Then decide on the best order for your paragraphs.
- Next, jot down one or two reasons or evidence to back up each main point.
- Use a text skeleton to plan your argument.

```
                                 reason, evidence or further
                                 detail to back up main point
          ┌──────────────┐
          │   1st main    │
          │    point      │
          └──────────────┘
                                 reason, evidence or further
                                 detail to back up main point
```

Stage 3

Now **draft your paragraphs**. Remember to:
- lay them out like a letter to a newspaper (for example, begin 'Sir or madam')
- use topic sentences and signposts to make the direction of the argument clear to the reader
- use formal language
- adopt a reasonable tone (emotive language is not suitable).

① Letter to Daniel

Aims

▶ Read a text by a reporter about his son, and past events in his life

▶ Explore how a writer uses descriptive detail to make key points (Wr11)

▶ Consider how a writer's point of view affects what he has to say (R11)

This text is written by BBC foreign correspondent Fergal Keane and takes the form of an imaginary letter for his new-born son.

We have called you Daniel Patrick but I've been told by my Chinese friends that you should have a Chinese name as well and this glorious dawn sky makes me think we'll call you Son of the Eastern Star. So that later, when you and I are far from Asia, perhaps standing on a beach

5   some evening, I can point at the sky and tell you of the Orient and the times and the people we knew there in the last years of the twentieth century.

Your coming has turned me upside down and inside out. So much that seemed essential to me has, in the past few days, taken on a different

10 colour. Like many foreign correspondents I know, I have lived a life that, on occasion, has veered close to the edge: war zones, natural disasters, darkness in all its shapes and forms.

In a world of insecurity and ambition and ego, it's easy to be drawn in, to take chances with our lives, to believe that what we do and what

15 people say about us is reason enough to gamble with death. Now, looking at your sleeping face, inches away from me, listening to your occasional sigh and gurgle, I wonder how I could have ever thought

glory and prizes and praise were sweeter than life.

And it's also true that I am pained, perhaps haunted is a better word,
by the memory, suddenly so vivid now, of each suffering child I have
come across on my journeys. To tell you the truth, it's nearly too much to
bear at this moment to even think of children being hurt and abused and
killed. And yet looking at you, the images come flooding back. Ten-year-
old Andi Mikail dying from napalm burns on a hillside in Eritrea, how
his voice cried out, growing ever more faint when the wind blew dust
onto his wounds. The two brothers, Domingo and Juste, in Menongue,
southern Angola. Juste, two years old and blind, dying from
malnutrition, being carried on seven-year-old Domingo's back. And
Domingo's words to me, 'He was nice before, but now he has the
hunger.'

Last October, in Afghanistan, when you were growing inside your
mother, I met Sharja, aged twelve. Motherless, fatherless, guiding me
through the grey ruins of her home, everything was gone, she told me.
And I knew that, for all her tender years, she had learned more about
loss than I would likely understand in a lifetime.

There is one last memory. Of Rwanda, and the churchyard of the
parish of Nyarabuye where, in a ransacked classroom, I found a mother
and her three young children huddled together where they'd been beaten
to death. The children had died holding on to their mother, that instinct
we all learn from birth and in one way or another cling to until we die.

Daniel, these memories explain some of the fierce protectiveness I feel
for you, the tenderness and the occasional moments of blind terror when
I imagine anything happening to you. But there is something more, a
story from long ago that I will tell you face to face, father to son, when
you are older. It's a very personal story but it's part of the picture. It has
to do with the long lines of blood and family, about our lives and how
we can get lost in them and, if we're lucky, find our way out again into
the sunlight.

It begins thirty-five years ago in a big city on a January morning with
snow on the ground and a woman walking to hospital to have her first
baby. She is in her early twenties and the city is still strange to her, bigger
and noisier than the easy streets and gentle hills of her distant home.
She's walking because there is no money and everything of value has
been pawned to pay for the alcohol to which her husband has become
addicted.

On the way, a taxi driver notices her sitting, exhausted and cold, in
the doorway of a shop and he takes her to hospital for free. Later that
day, she gives birth to a baby boy and, just as you are to me, he is the
best thing she has ever seen. Her husband comes that night and weeps
with joy when he sees his son. He is truly happy. Hungover, broke, but
in his own way happy, for they were both young and in love with each
other and their son.

Key Reading

Recount texts

This text is mainly in the form of a **recount**. Its **purpose** is to tell us about events that have happened.

The main features of this text are:

- It uses **paragraphs** to mark a **change of focus**. For example, the first paragraph deals with the naming of the baby.

- It includes **specific dates**, **times** and **names** of people and places, and uses **time connectives**; for example, '*Last October*, in *Afghanistan*, *when* you were growing inside your mother, I met *Sharja*, aged twelve…'

- It uses **descriptive language** to bring past events alive and convey strong emotions, such as adjectives, adverbs, powerful verbs, and sometimes imagery. For example, '…guiding me through the *grey ruins* of her home…'

1 This 'letter' is an imaginary one because Fergal Keane's son is only a baby, but it sounds like he is speaking to him. How does the **first paragraph** make us think this?

2 At the end of the text, the writer goes back even further in time. **How far back** does he go?

3 This is a particularly powerful and sad text, but it starts with a hopeful and pleasant image. **What is described** in the first paragraph?

Purpose

The purpose of this recount is to tell us about present – and past – events in a way that makes us think about some important issues.

 4 The writer tells us about the children he has met as a reporter. Discuss in a small group **why** you think this is.

Reading for meaning

5 Fergal Keane was a well established reporter when he wrote this. But he says:

> …looking at your sleeping face, inches away from me, listening to your occasional sigh and gurgle, I wonder how I could have ever thought glory and prizes and praise were sweeter than life.

How has his view about things **changed**?

BBC foreign correspondent Fergal Keane

The text is full of **contrasts** – when you write about the differences between two things or events. It also includes **comparisons** – when you write about what is similar or the same about two or more things.

R11

6 a) How does Fergal Keane compare his feelings to those of the mother and children he saw in Rwanda? Look carefully at the **words** he uses, particularly the **pronouns**.

b) He also mentions a girl called Sharja, whom he met in Afghanistan. In what ways is she **different** to him?

Focus on: Descriptive detail to make a point

Fergal Keane does not want to remember the terrible things he has seen as a reporter, but seeing his own son, he can't help it. So that we can understand how he feels, he tells us about:

> …ten-year-old Andi Mikail dying from napalm burns on a hillside in Eritrea, how his voice cried out, growing ever more faint when the wind blew dust onto his wounds.

The writing focuses on two **key senses** to convey the horror of what he saw – the sense of touch, and the sense of sound.

7 What are the **key senses** he uses below for this more pleasant description?

> …looking at your sleeping face, inches away from me, listening to your occasional sigh and gurgle, I wonder how I could have ever thought glory and prizes and praise were sweeter than life…

When we want to describe an experience, the strength of the adjectives we use is vital. For example, Keane describes the ten-year-old's voice 'growing ever more *faint*'.

Other adjectives for the level or type of sound could be 'loud', 'hoarse', 'quiet', 'powerful', 'low' or 'high', for example.

Or you could use adjectives of feeling, such as 'desperate', 'frightened', 'confused', 'relieved', 'joyous' or 'calm'.

8 Decide on **two adjectives** that best fit the spaces in the paragraph below, describing the sounds of villagers trapped on their roofs during a flood.

I could see the villagers clinging to the roofs. As the rescue helicopter got nearer I could hear their .... voices getting closer. Then, as we picked up the first survivor, I could hear his .... words to his wife: 'Don't worry – we'll be alright!'

Key Speaking and Listening

 9 The extract from Fergal Keane's letter is very sad and very powerful. Now imagine you are a BBC radio reporter with a family at home. You are away covering a war in another country and you find a child on his own. Fortunately, he is unhurt, but his family have been captured.

a) Write the **first paragraph of a report** for the six o'clock news on the radio. Remember to:

- describe the boy
- describe when and where you found him (use time connectives)
- recount what has happened to him
- use at least two key senses in your description to add detail and bring it alive.

You might start the report like this:

'Today, as we were returning to the hotel, we came across a ruined building. We got out of the jeep and crossed the road. At that moment, we heard...'

 b) Once you have written your paragraph, **read it out** to the rest of the class or smaller group. Try to vary the pace and feeling of your recount as a news reporter would.

② Runaway

Aims

▶ Read an extract from the opening to a novel about South Africa

▶ Review and develop reading skills related to finding information (R1)

▶ Use that information when responding to a text

▶ Write about a text in a considered way

In this extract from the novel *No Turning Back*, South African writer Beverley Naidoo tells a story based on the real-life tales of young children living on the streets.

Tiptoeing towards his mother's bed, Sipho touched the table to steady himself. He held his breath and glanced at the sleeping figures. Two grey shapes which could stir at any time. A small square of plastic above the bed let in the dim early morning light. His mother lay near the edge, one
5   hand resting over her rounded stomach. His stepfather was snoring heavily, a giant of a man stretched across the bed. Each snore shook the stillness of the tiny room. But it was a sigh from his mother that almost made him drop her bag and leave empty-handed. Then his fingers touched the coins. Grasping them, he turned and silently fled. Past the chipped
10 wooden table, the paraffin stove and the pot of cold porridge from the night before. Past his mattress on the floor with the crumpled blanket. Past the orange-crate cupboard and out of the door. He eased it shut, praying that the snoring would cover the sound of creaking hinges.

And then he ran. Keeping his head down, he weaved his way through
15 the patchwork of shacks in the smoky half-light, hoping against hope that no one would call his name. Thin chinks of yellow light and the smell of paraffin lamps behind the sheets of iron and wooden planks showed that people were beginning to rise. Ma and 'him' would have been getting up by now if they had work to go to. Sipho's heart was thumping against his
20 chest. It had been screwed up for the last few days, like the rest of his insides, as tight as a fist. But now it was going wild like the tail of a puppy just let out of a cage. He would have to get it under control before he got to the taxi rank.

Coming out from the shacks, he sprinted past the shop boarded up overnight. He could be seen more easily here. The quickest way would be to cut across by the men's hostel. But that was dangerous. Bullets whistling between the great grim building and the houses nearby had brought death to many people. No one knew when the fighting would start again and Ma had forbidden him to go near the place.

'That bullet won't stop to ask who you are,' Ma had said. But why should he listen to what Ma said any more? Still, it was safer to go the long way round, past his school.

Squares of misty light from houses on each side lit the way and, high above him, electric strips shone dully through the smoke. There were other people on the road already, most walking in the same direction. Sipho slowed down to a half-jog, half-walk. He might draw too much attention to himself if he ran. Passing the criss-cross wire fencing around the school, he shifted to the other side of the road. Even though the gate was locked, he could imagine the head teacher suddenly appearing from the low red-brick building and wanting to know where he was going.

The taxi rank was already humming with the early morning crowd milling alongside a line of minibuses. Pavement sellers had already set up their stalls. Some people in the queues carried bags and boxes, perhaps of things to sell in town themselves. With so many taxis, he had to make sure he got on the right one. Glancing briefly at a row of faces he noticed a woman looking at him. She had a baby on her back and seemed about Ma's age. No, he wouldn't ask her. Instead he moved away and asked a young man which was the right queue for Hillbrow.

'Take any one for Jo'burg city centre. It's that side.' The man pointed to where the crowd was thicker.

Slipping behind a line of people, Sipho was pleased he had managed to ask the question so smoothly. If only everyone would move along quickly so he could get inside the taxi. He kept his eyes trained in the direction of the school. What if Ma had woken up? She wouldn't feel up to coming after him, but she would wake his stepfather. If Ma sent him out looking for Sipho, he would be raging mad – even without a drink. Sipho could just imagine him storming through the crowd, shouting his name, demanding if anyone had seen a small boy aged twelve... a boy with big ears, the kind you can get hold of.

Sipho shivered, pulled his woollen cap down lower and clasped his arms around him. It was cold. He should have put on two jumpers.

Key Reading

Narrative texts

This text is a **narrative**. Its **purpose** is to tell a story in an interesting and entertaining way.

The main features of this text are:

- It has a **structure** which includes an **introduction** (the development, complication, climax and resolution of the plot all come later). This opening introduces the main situation and events. For example, the text follows Sipho as he secretly leaves his home.

- It features clearly drawn **characters** in Sipho, his Ma and stepfather, and a **narrator**, who tells the story in either the first person (I/we) or the third person (he/she/it), for example, 'Sipho touched the table to steady himself. *He* held his breath…'

- The **characters' feelings** are shown or **implied** through the narrative rather than stated directly, for example, '…he turned and *silently fled*', might suggest Sipho is feeling guilty.

- It uses **expressive and descriptive language**, such as powerful verbs, nouns, adjectives and figurative language, for example, '…he *weaved* his way through the *patchwork of shacks* in the *smoky half-light*.'

1 The opening paragraph sets the scene for us. **Find descriptions** for each of the following:

   a) the size of the room

   b) the food left over from the night before

   c) a damaged item of furniture.

2 Apart from Sipho, Ma and the stepfather, **two other characters** are briefly mentioned. Who are they?

•••••••••••••••••••••••••••••••••

Purpose

Of course, Beverley Naidoo's *main* purpose is to tell a good story. During the opening she does this by raising questions in the reader's mind. The main question is: 'Why is Sipho running away from home?'.

3 In pairs, look through the text again and discuss what you think the **answer** to this question is.
Find **evidence** in the extract to support your views. For example, if your answer is: 'Sipho hates his mother', identify where it says or implies this.

Be careful – you may find evidence, but it might have more than one meaning. For example, does the following evidence from the extract necessarily prove that his mother has done something really bad to him?

> But why should he listen to what Ma said any more?

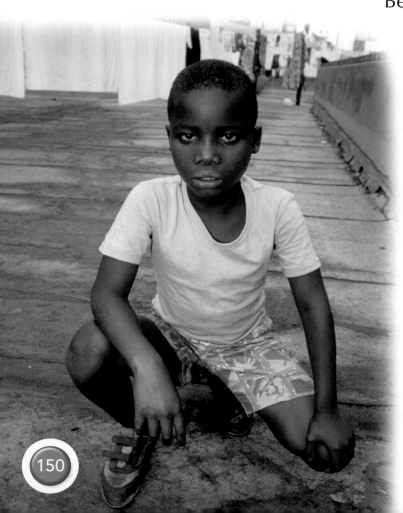

Reading for meaning

Writers often like to give a clear idea of a place or setting at the start of a narrative. In fact, in this opening we are told quite a lot about where Sipho lives. What can we **infer** about Sipho's life from this information?

> **imply** suggest or hint at a meaning that is not obvious
>
> **infer** work out or deduce a meaning

R1   **4** Copy and **complete the table** below, adding your own ideas to column 3.

Reference	Where	What we can infer
'A small square of plastic above the bed let in the dim early morning light.'	Paragraph 1	No proper windows in the house
'the orange-crate cupboard…'	Paragraph 1	The family are…
'shop boarded up overnight…'	Paragraph 3	There's a lot of…
'Bullets whistling…'	Paragraph 3	

• •

Focus on: Adding quotations to your writing

When you are writing about texts, either in class or in a test situation, you need to provide evidence for what you write.

So, using the table you completed for question 4, we could write:

'The writer tells us that Sipho's home has a 'small square of plastic above the bed'. This suggests that Sipho's house does not have proper windows and that his family is poor.'

Notice that in this example the actual words **(quotation)** from the text have **inverted commas** (speech marks) around them. This is to make sure the reader knows these come from the original text. It is *not* because they are spoken in this case.

Also notice that the writer finishes by telling us *what we can infer* from this quotation.

> **Grammar for reading**
>
> A **quotation** is the name for words we have removed from a text to make a point.

S4 **5** Practise using **quotations** with these two example sentences.

a) Add the missing **inverted commas** around the quotation (you will need to check the text):

We can tell that Sipho is worried that the door will make a noise because he mentions its creaking hinges.

b) Find a **suitable quotation** to add to this sentence (see the first paragraph):

It is clear that Sipho's stepfather is very large because he is described as a 'a ....'

Key Writing

R1 **6 a)** Check through the last half of the text to find any references to **buildings** or the **setting**. Add these to the table you started for question 4.

Make sure you also include what you **infer** from each detail in the third column. For example, don't just say that Sipho doesn't have proper windows, add what this tells us.

b) Write two paragraphs about what we find out from the text about Sipho's home and the area he lives in. Paragraph 1 should be about his home and paragraph 2 should be about his neighbourhood.

You could start them like this:
Paragraph 1: Sipho's home is...
Paragraph 2: His home is situated in a...

Remember to:
- support what you say with **quotations**
- put the quotations inside **inverted commas**.

③ Tiger tracking in Rajasthan

Aims

▶ Read an information text about tigers in Rajasthan, India

▶ Look at how to adjust your style to suit purpose and audience

▶ Explore how writers bring together different types of information (Wr9)

▶ Write an information text for a different audience (S9)

In this extract about another land, the tiger takes centre stage. But man's influence is never far away...

Lying 109 miles (176 km) southwest of Bharatpur, near the town of Sawai Madhopur and at the junction of the Aravalli and Vindhya ranges, Ranthambore National Park is one of the best places in the world to see tigers in the wild. This 198 square mile (513 km²) park, once the private hunting grounds of the
5   maharajas of Jaipur, became a national park in 1973 as part of Project Tiger. The road into the park winds through a steep desert canyon opening onto a region of marshes, streams, lakes, grasslands and craggy hills. Much of the area is covered by
10 virgin deciduous forests studded with palms. Mango groves and huge banyans grow around the lakes.

    On drives in open-sided jeeps, you'll see abundant wildlife, including sambars (large deer), Indian gazelles, langur monkeys, blue bucks, sloth bears, marsh crocodiles and Indian flying foxes.
15 The tigers are elusive, and sightings can never be guaranteed, but, with luck, you may experience the thrill of seeing a tigress with her young as you wind through the forest in the early morning or late afternoon. You'll certainly see a wide range of birds, including paradise flycatchers, green pigeons, pheasant-
20 tailed jaçanas, white wagtails, and even crested serpent eagles.

Jogi Mahal, the former hunting lodge of the maharajas, overlooks the main marsh, Padam Talao, where painted storks and spotted deer feed. At night here, you may hear the scream of a leopard or the hoot of an eagle owl. The massive Ranthambore Fort, built in the tenth century and located on a ridge-top in the park's southwestern corner, affords a spectacular panoramic view. Throughout the park you'll see remnants of the past: pavilions, tombs and hunting blinds. Allow at least three days here in order to make the most of your visit.

India's national parks are islands of native habitat in a country where the pressures of population are making ever-growing demands for farming land. Remarkably, over 300 parks covering 35,000 square miles (90,000 km^2) have been set aside to protect endangered species and habitats. There have, however, been significant disputes, and unless India's population growth is curbed, the demand for food may become too great to save these preserves.

In 1973, Project Tiger was launched in India to protect and rehabilitate tiger populations in nine sanctuaries and national parks with a variety of habitats. Hunting these magnificent cats has been banned since that time and, as a result, tiger numbers have increased from 1,800 to about 4,000.

There are now eight tiger preserves throughout the country. Much has been learned about tigers by biologists, particularly in Ranthambore, where the tigers are thriving under protection: Tigers here are no longer afraid of humans and are often seen padding about in broad daylight. Previously it was thought that they were strictly nocturnal. Project Tiger has saved tigers from extinction, but corruption in local management, poaching, and pressures for timber and grazing land pose major threats to their habitat, particularly in times of drought.

hunting blinds small structures designed to conceal hunters, also known as hides

Key Reading

Information texts

This text is an **information** text. Its **purpose** is to provide information in order to help us understand a place and some related issues.

The main features of this text are:

● It has an **introduction** with a **general statement**, followed by **logical sections** with **specific facts**, for example, the first paragraph mentions the name of the park, and that it is 'one of the best places in the world to see tigers in the wild'.

● It uses the **present tense** to describe how things are, for example, 'Mango groves and huge banyans *grow* around the lakes.'

● It uses **formal and impersonal language**, for example, 'The massive Ranthambore Fort, built in the tenth century and located on a ridge-top in the park's southwestern corner, affords a spectacular panoramic view.'

● It uses **technical** or subject-related **language**, for example, 'tiger populations', 'sanctuaries', 'a variety of habitats'.

1 What is the **second paragraph** mainly about?

2 The first paragraph is full of **geographical terms** and references. List as many as you can.

Purpose

On the surface, this seems to be a simple information text. It tells us about the national park and the creatures that can be seen there. Is there a message behind this information, however?

3 a) Read these two quotations from the final two paragraphs:

- ● 'Hunting these magnificent cats has been banned.'
- ● 'Project Tiger has saved tigers from extinction, but corruption in local management, poaching, and pressures for timber and grazing land pose major threats to their habitat.'

b) In pairs, discuss what **viewpoint** or **opinion** you think we are being given about tigers and their situation from these examples.

A tiger being tagged

157

Reading for meaning

4 Although this is an information text, the writer makes it sound as if Rajasthan is a place worth visiting. Look at the extracts from paragraph 2 below. Which of these **words** suggest a trip to the park will be worthwhile?

> On drives in open-sided jeeps, you'll see abundant wildlife…

> …sightings can never be guaranteed, but, with luck, you may experience the thrill of seeing a tigress with her young as you wind through the forest in the early morning or late afternoon…

5 The writer adds a wealth of detail about the park by giving specific facts. In particular, he uses lists to show the wide range of geographical features, animals and birdlife the park holds.

a) Identify **three of these lists** in paragraphs 1 and 2.

b) What **effect** would these have on a reader thinking of visiting the park?

Focus on: Integrating information

The first paragraph of the text provides clear factual information:

size

what it is and who owned it

> This 198 square mile (513 km^2) park, once the private hunting grounds of the maharajas of Jaipur, became a national park in 1973…

its history/background

However, if the text was just factual information using mostly dates and figures, its interest would be limited. So, the writer also provides us with information we can **visualise** (see in our minds) about the park:

> The road into the park winds through a steep desert canyon opening onto a region of marshes, streams, lakes, grasslands and craggy hills.

 6 Below is another set of information about another national park. Sort points A–G into **two lists**:

- list 1, which **provides mostly figures** and **dates**
- list 2, which provides information that creates an **image** in our minds.

A   Bharatpur, one of Rajasthan's four national parks
B   Consists of lakes and canals fed by local rivers
C   Located 33 miles west of Agra
D   Shallow marshes provide wintering sites for birds
E   11 square miles (29 km^2) in area
F   Large thorny acacia trees line the paths
G   350 species of birds

Key Writing

7 Take the information from lists 1 and 2 and turn it into **two paragraphs**:

● Paragraph 1 should be about the facts and figures.

● Paragraph 2 should be about the landscape and produce an image in the readers' minds.

You will need to make proper sentences from the lettered points by…

● adding or changing words

● using link words (connectives or conjunctions such as 'and' or 'where') between the sentences.

Paragraph 1 could begin like this:

> Bharatpur is one of Rajasthan's four national parks, and…

added word to make a sentence

conjunction links to next bit of information

8 If you were writing this information for **younger children**, several words might need to be replaced or removed.

a) What words could you use instead of…

● 'consists of'

● 'located'

● 'provide'?

b) Which details might need to be removed or explained?

④ Unit 7 Assignment: Himalaya correspondent

Assessment Focus

▶ **AF3** Organise and present whole texts effectively, sequencing and structuring information, ideas and events

> **You**: are a journalist who writes articles for a magazine about remote places and people.
>
> **Your task**: to write about the Himalayas and threats to the environment.

Stage 1

Here are the notes you made during your research.

- Himalayas: more than 1,600 miles (2,600 km) in size from west to east
- Some countries they go through: Pakistan, India, Tibet, Nepal and Bhutan
- The Great Himalaya chain in Nepal and Tibet has highest mountains, with Mount Everest at 29,028 feet (8,854m) being the highest
- Lots of rubbish along the trails – the worst at top of Everest
- 200,000 tourists visit Nepal each year
- Hillsides are eroding because firewood needed to keep trekkers and porters warm
- 77,000 trekking permits issued each year
- Nepalese businessman plans to open a cyber-café halfway up Everest
- Most animals seen tend to be domestic ones – yaks, goats and chickens
- Sometimes langur monkeys and monal pheasants can be seen on lower forest trails
- Higher up, golden eagles and elusive snow leopards might be seen
- Some group treks now come just to clean up rubbish on trails.

Sort these points into **two lists**. List 1 is mainly concerned with facts and figures, while list 2 is concerned with what can be seen, and the problems and other issues.

Stage 2

Decide on a **title** for your article. Then organise your two lists into **four paragraphs**. You could follow this structure:

Paragraph 1: Information about the Himalayas, where they are, etc.

Paragraph 2: Information about the number of travellers, walkers, trekkers, etc.

Paragraph 3: The wildlife that can be found

Paragraph 4: Problems and issues.

Stage 3

Draft your information text, using your plan as a guide.

● Use **connectives** and **conjunctions** to link your ideas, and say as much as you can.

● Think carefully about the **formality** of the language. Although this text will present some of the problems of the Himalayas, this is not a personal piece, so do not use the first person ('I'). Model your work on the style of the text on pages 154–155.

● Use the **present tense**.

● Include **technical terms** where they to help present information.

Challenge

Use the Internet or your school library to access some images of the Himalayas to **illustrate your article**. Add some captions to the images (short descriptions that go underneath the images). Put your text and images together as one article.

① The salt marshes

Aims

▸ Read an extract from *The Woman in Black*

▸ Learn to identify different layers of meaning in a text (W7)

▸ Identify shifts of mood and how these are linked across paragraphs (S6)

▸ Write a series of linked paragraphs

This extract comes from *The Woman in Black* by Susan Hill. Arthur Kipps, a solicitor, is returning from the funeral of Mrs Alice Drablow. Her house – Eel Marsh House – looks out on the lonely and dangerous salt marshes and is linked to the mainland by Nine Lives Causeway.

On the causeway path it was still quite dry underfoot but to my left I saw that the water had begun to seep nearer, quite silent now, quite slow. I wondered how deeply the path went under water when the tide was at its height. But on a still night such as this, there was plenty of time to cross in safety, though the distance was greater, now I was traversing it on foot, than it had seemed when we trotted over in Keckwick's pony cart, and the end of the causeway path seemed to be receding into the greyness ahead. I had never been quite so alone, nor felt quite so small and insignificant in a vast landscape before, and I fell into a not unpleasant brooding, philosophical frame of mind, struck by the absolute indifference of water and sky to my presence.

Some minutes later, I could not tell how many, I came out of my reverie, to realize that I could no longer see very far in front of me and when I turned around I was startled to find that Eel Marsh House, too, was invisible, not because the darkness of evening had fallen, but because of a thick, damp sea-mist that had come rolling over the marshes and enveloped everything, myself, the house behind me, the end of the causeway path and the countryside ahead. It was a mist like a damp clinging cobwebby thing, fine and yet impenetrable…I felt confused, teased by it, as though it were made up of millions of live fingers that crept over me, hung on me and then shifted away again. Above 20 all, it was the suddenness of it that had so unnerved and disorientated me.

For a short time, I walked slowly on, determined to stick to my path until I came out onto the safety of the country road. But it began to dawn upon me that I should as likely as not become very quickly lost once I had left the straightness of the causeway, and might wander all night in exhaustion. The most obvious and 25 sensible course was to turn and retrace my steps the few hundred yards I had come and to wait at the house until either the mist cleared or Keckwick arrived to fetch me, or both.

That walk back was a nightmare. I was obliged to go step by slow step, for fear of 30 veering off onto the marsh, and then into the rising water. If I looked up or around me, I was at once baffled by the moving, shifting mist, and so on I stumbled, praying to reach the house, which was farther away than I had imagined. Then somewhere away in the swirling mist and dark, I heard the sound that lifted my heart, the distant but unmistakable clip-clop of the pony's hooves and the rumble and creak of the trap. So Keckwick was unperturbed by the mist, quite used to 35 travelling through the lanes and across the causeway in darkness, and I stopped and waited to see a lantern – for surely he must carry one – and half wondered whether to shout and make my presence known, in case he came suddenly upon me and ran me down into the ditch.

Then I realised that the mist played tricks with sound as well as sight, for not 40 only did the noise of the trap stay further away from me for longer than I might have expected but also it seemed to come not from directly behind me, straight down the causeway path, but instead to be away to my right, out on the marsh. I tried to work out the direction of the wind but there was none. I turned around but then the sound began to recede further away again. Baffled, I stood and waited, 45 straining to listen through the mist. What I heard next chilled and horrified me, even though I could neither understand nor account for it. The noise of the pony trap grew fainter then stopped abruptly and away on the marsh was a curious draining, sucking, churning sound, which went on, together with the shrill neighing and whinnying of a horse in panic, and then I heard another cry, a shout, a terrified 50 sobbing – it was hard to decipher – but with horror I realized that it came from a child, a young child. I stood absolutely helpless in the mist that clouded me and everything from my sight, almost weeping in an agony of fear and frustration, and I knew that I was hearing, beyond any doubt, appalling last noises of a pony and trap, carrying a child in it, as well as whatever adult – presumably Keckwick – was 55 driving and was even now struggling desperately. It had somehow lost the causeway path and fallen into the marshes and was being dragged under by the quicksand and the pull of the incoming tide.

I began to yell until I thought my lungs would burst…

trap a small two-wheeled carriage pulled by a horse or pony
causeway a road or track that runs across low or wet ground, sometimes connecting an island with the mainland
philosophical deeply thoughtful
reverie daydream
traversing crossing

Key Reading

Narrative texts

This text is a story or **narrative**. The **purpose** of a narrative is to entertain us.

The main features of this text are:

- It has a structure that includes an **introduction**, a **complication**, a **crisis** and a **resolution** (conclusion) when things are sorted out. The opening of a text may introduce a setting, an event or a character.

- It has a **narrator**, who tells the story in either the first person (I/we) or the third person, for example, '*I* was obliged to go step by slow step…'

- It uses **powerful and descriptive language**, to maintain the interest of the reader, for example, 'I was *startled* to find that Eel Marsh House, too, was *invisible*…'

1 What are the **main events** in the extract? Think about what happens to Arthur and what he hears.

2 a) Is this a **first-** or a **third-person narrative**? Find three pieces of evidence for your answer in paragraph 1.

b) What **tense** is the story told in?

Purpose

The purpose of a narrative is to entertain us.

3 a) In pairs, decide whether the extract is from:

- a fantasy
- a ghost story
- crime fiction
- historical fiction.

b) Taking your answer into account, why do you think the writer wrote the story? Think of **two reasons**.

4 At the end of the extract, what do you think

- will happen to Arthur
- has happened to Keckwick?

Reading for meaning

When we begin reading the extract we quickly gain a sense that something unfortunate might happen. Study the opening sentence:

> On the causeway path it was still quite dry underfoot but to my left I saw that the water had begun to seep nearer, quite silent now, quite slow.

a dangerous path

path very slowly being engulfed by the tide

5 a) How does Arthur feel about the **safety** of the causeway to begin with? Find the exact words in paragraph 1 that tell you.

b) What do you think of Arthur's decision to cross the causeway?

c) At this point in the extract, what do you **infer** might happen to him?

infer work out or deduce
imply suggest or hint at a meaning that is no obvious

167

6 Near the beginning of paragraph 2, **what else happens** to make Arthur's situation worse?

W7

7 So far you should have been able to work out that Arthur is in danger from the rising tide and the mist. However, something deeper is **implied** towards the end of paragraph 2. Read the following sentences:

> It was a mist like a damp clinging cobwebby thing, fine and yet impenetrable… I felt confused, teased by it, as though it were made up of millions of live fingers that crept over me, hung on me and then shifted away again.

a) In pairs, **make a note of all the words** that suggest the mist is creepier than it first seems.

b) Then discuss what else could be happening to Arthur. Think of at least **two possibilities** and write down your answer.

Focus on: The mood

The mood or **tone** of a piece of writing is the kind of feeling created. When tension is building up in a story, new paragraphs often signal an increase in mood or shifts of mood, as well as giving information. This is true in this text.

S6, R3

8 Look back at the example sentence in question 7. Here we could say that the mood created is one of concern.

Now look at paragraph 2. In this paragraph concern has become anxiety. The mist has descended and Arthur is in greater danger. Words such as 'startled' indicate this.

a) **Draw up a table** like the one below. In pairs, write in column 1 the first sentence (or the sentence signpost) for each paragraph, which shows the key idea.

b) Next, discuss what kind of **mood** is created in each paragraph, and why. Note any build-up in tension or shift of mood. Record your thoughts in column 2 of your table. Follow the example provided. Some useful words have been provided to help you.

Sentence signpost	Mood created
Paragraph 1: 'On the causeway path it was still quite dry underfoot but to my left I saw that the water had begun to seep nearer...'	concern – something unfortunate could happen

Useful words

fear   confusion   composure   worry   desperation

terror   panic   dread   surprise   frustration

Key Writing

When Arthur first sees remote Eel Marsh House in its desolate landscape, he is amazed by its 'mysterious shimmering beauty'. But inside it is an eerie, unwelcoming place. In an attempt to dispel his unease he wanders from room to room switching on all the lights, until he comes to a locked door. Try as he might, he cannot open it.

9 Put yourself in Arthur's shoes and imagine you are visiting Eel Marsh House. **Write about your experiences in three paragraphs** following this plan:

Paragraph 1: I see the house from a distance set against the marshes and am keen to look inside.

Paragraph 2: I enter and my mood changes.

Paragraph 3: I move from room to room becoming more and more frightened. I try to open the locked door. (Do I succeed? How do I escape?)

Remember to:

- narrate the tale in the **first person**
- use the **past tense**
- link your paragraphs using **sentence signposts** to build up tension and to signal changes of mood
- include **powerful verbs, nouns, adjectives and adverbs** in your descriptions. For example: 'solitude', 'musty', 'gloomy', 'echo', 'warning', 'stealthily', 'crept', 'stumbled', 'frantic', 'shuddered'.

② Fears and phobias

- Read an information text about fears and phobias
- Examine the layout features of a text and how and why you might change them (Wr4)
- Study an example that is used to explain a point
- Study how modal verbs help us to explore possibilities
- Redraft an information text

This webpage is taken from a self-help health website.

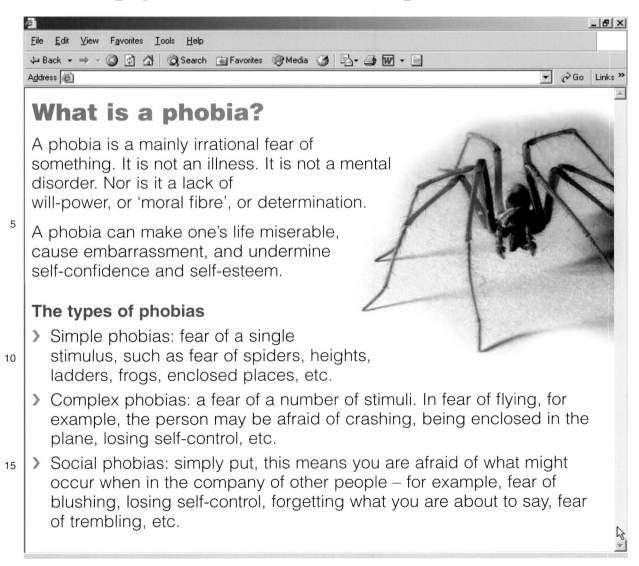

What is a phobia?

A phobia is a mainly irrational fear of something. It is not an illness. It is not a mental disorder. Nor is it a lack of will-power, or 'moral fibre', or determination.

5 A phobia can make one's life miserable, cause embarrassment, and undermine self-confidence and self-esteem.

The types of phobias

> Simple phobias: fear of a single
10 stimulus, such as fear of spiders, heights, ladders, frogs, enclosed places, etc.

> Complex phobias: a fear of a number of stimuli. In fear of flying, for example, the person may be afraid of crashing, being enclosed in the plane, losing self-control, etc.

15 > Social phobias: simply put, this means you are afraid of what might occur when in the company of other people – for example, fear of blushing, losing self-control, forgetting what you are about to say, fear of trembling, etc.

> Panic attacks: a panic attack can be a quite terrifying ordeal unless you
20 understand what is going on and why it is going on. Panics are very
common and appear mainly to affect people who normally give the
impression of being confident, reliable and dependable.

> Agoraphobia: Literally 'fear of the market place' and, up to a decade or
so ago, the term was used to describe people who were afraid of open
25 spaces. 'Agoraphobia' is now used to describe those who experience
increasing nervousness the further they travel from their own home. In
severe cases they may not venture from home at all.

The difference between a fear and a phobia

The distinction generally made is to say that a fear is rational and that
30 when fear becomes irrational it is a phobia.

In reality the difference is mainly one of degree and the handiest way to
distinguish them is by saying that a phobia is different from a fear by
being more irrational. Because, having been fuelled by our imagination,
every fear will have a degree of irrationality to it.

Irrational fear
35

A phobia is an irrational fear – which is why someone who is phobic will
often say 'I know it's silly, but… ' They are quite well aware that, while
there may be some rational basis for their fear, it is largely irrational.

Take the example of a phobia of snakes. If you live in the United Kingdom
40 there is a slight possibility that you may be out in the countryside on a
warm summer's day and you may possibly come across one of our
increasingly rare adders, and you just might not see it, and it might be so
unaware of your very silent approach that it doesn't quietly slip away, and
you might possibly be walking about without wearing shoes, and you
45 might possibly step on it and get bitten.

All of this is not very likely, I agree, but it is just possible. And therefore a
UK resident has some reason to be fearful of snakes.

Yet, while the likelihood of being bitten by an adder in the UK is very
small, someone who is afraid of snakes can be so fearful that they cannot
50 even pass a pet shop just in case there may be snakes on display in the
window. They may even have to leave the room if snakes are featured on
the television. Or be unable to look at a picture of snakes in a magazine.

Key Reading

Information texts

This text is mainly an **information text**. Its **purpose** is to give clear information about a topic.

The main features of this text are:

- It uses the **present tense** when it is telling things as they are, for example, 'A phobia *is* a mainly irrational fear…'

- The **layout** of the text includes **headings and subheadings** to make it easier to find information and allow the reader to browse, for example, 'The Types of Phobia'.

- It includes **technical language** related to the topic. For example, 'complex phobias', 'social phobias', 'agoraphobia'.

- It features a **general statement** that introduces the topic, followed by **specific facts**.

1 What **tense** is the text mainly written in? Find three examples from different paragraphs.

2 From what **point of view** (in what 'person') is it mainly written?

3 Look through the text again. Which **layout features** help you to find the information quickly?

4 Some of the **technical terms** are easier to understand than others. Find two examples that you can understand easily.

Purpose

5 a) In pairs, discuss whether the **main purpose** of this text is:
- to give information about phobias
- to explain what a phobia is
- to advise how to cope with phobias
- to tell you how to get rid of a phobia.

Provide evidence for your choice.

b) Do any of the other purposes above also suit this text?

6 Most information texts are written in a formal style, but this one uses a **chatty style** in many paragraphs. Why might this be?

Reading for meaning

The layout of the text, using subheadings, means the reader can browse the text – paying attention to some parts and ignoring others. However, under each subheading the paragraphs can contain a great deal of information.

Wr4

7 In a small group, work out how you could add to or change the text to make it:
- easier to find information
- more attractive.

a) Look through the whole text from the opening statement to the final paragraph.
- Share ideas and **discuss** their usefulness.
- Reject some ideas and retain others.

You could start your discussion by saying why you **agree or disagree** with the following statements:
- Using more subheadings might be useful.
- Illustrations would not be useful in this kind of text.

b) Choose someone to **record at least four points** of your group's best ideas.

● ●

Focus on: Making a point clear

Under the subheading 'Irrational fear', an example is given that helps us to understand the difference between a fear and phobia. The example reads like a story, using modal verbs to suggest what might happen:

modal verb

> Take the example of a phobia of snakes. If you live in the United Kingdom there is a slight possibility that you may be out in the countryside on a warm summer's day and you may possibly come across one of our increasingly rare adders, and you just might not see it, and it might be so unaware of your very silent approach that it doesn't quietly slip away, and you might possibly be walking about without wearing shoes, and you might possibly step on it and get bitten.

8 **a)** Find the other **modal verbs** in the paragraph as you read through.

b) What is the **conclusion** of the paragraph? In other words, what might happen to you?

9 **a)** Now study the paragraph below. It sums up the point of the example. What is it? Write it down **in your own words**.

> All of this is not very likely, I agree, but it is just possible. And therefore a UK resident has some reason to be fearful of snakes.

b) What **connective** is used to make the point?

10 Decide what the **difference in meaning** is between:

- a rational fear
- an irrational fear.

(If you need to, read the information under the subheading 'The difference between a fear and a phobia' again.)

Grammar for reading

Modal verbs, such as 'should', 'would', 'could', 'might' and 'may', help us to think about the likelihood of different possibilities.

Key Writing

11 Working in pairs, **rewrite the information** under the subheading 'The types of phobias' and present it in a user-friendly way. To do this you will need to:

- cut back the information about each phobia, whilst making sure you keep the correct definitions
- use simpler, more informal language
- reduce the number of examples given for each phobia.

Your changed version of the first phobia might look like this:

highlight in bold   **change to informal language, such as, 'one thing'**

> Simple phobias: fear of a single stimulus such as fear of heights, or ladders, frogs, enclosed places, etc.

change punctuation   **cut examples**   **add useful words**

The first phobia example would now read:

> Simple Phobias: fear of one thing, such as fear of heights or ladders.

What other **layout features** could you use to improve this example? Think back to the discussion and the notes your group made under question 7.

To Kill a Mockingbird

▶ Read an extract from the play of *To Kill A Mockingbird* (R14)

▶ Learn about the importance of stage directions

▶ Study the same extract in the novel

▶ Discuss the differences between the two extracts (R10)

To Kill A Mockingbird is a novel written by Harper Lee and set in the southern states of America during the 1930s. This extract from the play (based on the novel and written by Christopher Sergal) involves Scout Finch and her older brother Jem. The character called Jean is Scout as an adult, looking back and commenting on the action.

> (As they go into the house, the light begins to dim except for a small isolated light on JEAN. As she speaks, the light continues to dim until the stage is entirely dark except for her, and she is only dimly seen.)
>
> 5 JEAN: Atticus was underestimating what anger and sick frustration could do to an already unbalanced man. The night we found out — there was a pageant at the school auditorium and Jem said that he'd take me. It was to be our longest journey together. Wind was coming up and Jem
> 10 said it might be raining before we got home. Heavy clouds had blacked out the moon, and it was pitch dark. Before we left, Cal had a pinprick of apprehension. When I asked what was the matter, she said 'Somebody just walked over my grave.' On the way to school, Jem had a flashlight.
>
> 15 (At this JEM turns on a pinpoint flashlight, directing it into SCOUT's face.)
>
> JEM (teasing):   You scared? Scared of haints?
>
> SCOUT (scornfully): Haints, hot steams, incantations, secret signs — I'm too old.

20	JEM (*reciting*):	'Angel bright, life-in-death, get off the road, don't suck my breath.'
	SCOUT (*sharply*):	Cut it out!
	JEM:	You're scared now because we're passin' Boo Radley's place.
25	SCOUT:	I'm *not* scared. 'Sides he must not be home.
	JEM:	How c'n ya tell?
	SCOUT (*logically*):	If he was, there wouldn't be a bird singing in the Radley tree. Hear that
30		mocker?

(As they listen to the birdsong, the flashlight goes out.)

	SCOUT:	Turn on the light again.
	JEM:	Something wrong with it. C'mon. Gimme your hand.

(They start to go.)

35		
	SCOUT:	How do you know where we're at?
	JEM:	I can tell we under the tree now because we're passing through a cool spot. (*As they are going offstage*) Careful.
40	JEAN:	The trip back from the pageant was more eventful. The moon had been in and out of the heavy rainclouds, but as we started home it was black dark – and there was the stillness that sometimes comes before a thunderstorm. (*Her voice becoming increasingly involved.*) Jem thought he heard something, and we stopped to listen. Then we walked a few more steps, and he stopped again. I thought he was trying to scare me, but that wasn't it. He held my hand tight and pulled me along fast. Then we stopped suddenly.
45		
50		
55		
60		

(There are sounds of several steps being taken, and then they stop.)

JEAN: I thought I heard steps following, too.

65 *(There is a rumble of distant thunder. SCOUT speaks to JEM in the darkness. The light on JEAN has dimmed away. The stage is in total darkness.)*

SCOUT *(voice in the darkness)*:
                        Jem, are you afraid?

JEM *(voice)*:   Think we're not too far to the tree
70   now.

SCOUT: Reckon we ought to sing, Jem.

JEM *(worried)*:   No. Be real quiet, Scout.

(There is another rumble of thunder.)

SCOUT: Just the thunderstorm gettin' closer.

75 JEM *(more worried)*: No, not that - Listen!

(There is the sound of someone running toward them.)

SCOUT *(with sudden alarm)*:
                        I hear! Jem!

JEM *(shouting imperatively)*:
80   He's coming! Run, Scout! Run! Run!

SCOUT *(in trouble)*: I tripped! Jem - help me!

JEM: Get away, Scout - Run!

*(Then JEM cries out as someone grabs him. There is a sound of struggling. A man's voice is heard - angry,
85 unintelligible.)*

ATTACKER: Got 'cha - now you'll - damn ya -
                        show 'em.

(There is a crack and JEM screams with pain.)

Atticus (Finch) Scout and Jem's lawyer father
Cal (Calpurnia) The Finch's black housekeeper
Boo (Arthur) Radley a neighbour, nervous and withdrawn
haints ghosts
mocker mockingbird

Key Reading

Play scripts

This text is a **play script**. Its **purpose** is to provide a written version for those involved in a play's performance and production. It can also be used for classroom study.

The main features of this text are:

● Its **layout**, which features text divided into scenes, names of characters on the left (in capitals), words of characters following after names.

● It presents **visual information/directions** in italics. These can describe a scene or a character's actions. In this extract the **stage directions** are detailed and sometimes lengthy. They are written in italics within brackets.

● The **dialogue/speech** is not placed within inverted commas. The dialogue in plays is often written in short sentences so that it sounds like ordinary speech. (However, Jean's **commentary** is long because she is giving the audience information.) For example:

'JEM *(more worried)* No, not that – Listen!'

1 **Where** are the children going to and coming back from?

2 Jem treats Scout differently in both scenes. How?

3 What is the **weather** like and what time of day is it? Why does this suit what is happening in the extract?

4 Find two **stage directions** that show a change in Jem's mood.

5 Why can't **Jean** help the children?

Purpose

A play tells a story on stage and must entertain its **audience**. At the centre of the action there is usually **conflict** between one or more of the characters.

6 The **main conflict** in this extract is very dramatic. What is it? And where does it happen?

7 This play script has been adapted from a novel and has a **particular audience** in mind. Who do you think the audience is? Provide a reason for your answer.

Reading for meaning

R14

8 a) The extract is divided into two short parts or scenes. The first depicts Scout and Jem on their way to the school pageant. What do the stage directions below tell you about **Jem's attitude** to Scout? How does she react?

```
JEM (teasing):        You scared? Scared of haints?

SCOUT (scornfully):   Haints, hot steams, incantations,
                      secret signs – I'm too old.

JEM (reciting):       'Angel bright, life-in-death, get off
                      the road, don't suck my breath.'

SCOUT (sharply):      Cut it out!
```

b) In pairs, **read the lines** with expression, adopting a role each.

c) The second part depicts the return journey. Find this in the script and look carefully at the stage directions. Then **choose four or five lines**. Adopt the same roles again and read the lines with expression.

9 **a)** Focus on the **character of Scout**. Discuss with your partner what Scout is afraid of in part 1 and in part 2 of the script.

b) There is a clear difference between Scout's fears in the two parts. In the first, on the way to the pageant, her fears are not based on anything real. The words below describe this type of fear. (Check the meanings in a dictionary if you need to.)

> **Scout's Fears**
> **Part 1**
> imagined   fantastical   impossible
> superstitious   irrational

With your partner, **draw up a list** of words that describe her fears on the return journey under the heading 'Scout's Fears, Part 2'. Use a dictionary and a thesaurus.

10 **a)** With your partner use your lists of words to **sum up** the different kinds of fear that Scout experiences.

b) Then, on your own, **write a paragraph** of about 75 words to explain the difference in her fears. Refer to evidence from the script.

Focus on: From novel to play

11 When a writer adapts a play from a novel they have to make many changes. But some things also stay the same. On the next page is the extract from the novel about Scout and Jem's return from the pageant.

a) Before studying the annotations **read the extract** from the novel and find the part in the script where this occurs.

b) The annotations show a few of the similarities and differences between the two. Find **two other differences** between the extracts from the play and the novel.

dialogue very similar to the script

begins a detailed description of the journey home

weather different in the play

'You reckon we oughta sing, Jem?'
'No. be real quiet again, Scout.'
We had not increased our pace. Jem knew as well as I that it was difficult to walk fast without stumping a toe, tripping on stones, and other inconveniences, and I was barefooted. Maybe it was the wind rustling the trees. But there wasn't any wind and there wasn't any trees except the big oak.

Our company shuffled and dragged his feet, as if wearing heavy shoes. Whoever it was wore thick cotton pants; what I thought were trees rustling was the soft swish of cotton on cotton, wheek, wheek, with every step.

I felt the sand go cold under my feet and I knew we were near the big oak. Jem pressed my head. We stopped and listened.

Shuffle-foot had not stopped with us this time. His trousers swished softly and steadily. Then they stopped. He was running, running towards us with no child's steps.

'Run, Scout! Run! Run!' Jem screamed.

begins a detailed description of the attacker

Key Speaking and Listening

 12 **a)** In a group of four, **discuss the following questions:**

- After reading the extract from the novel why do you think stage directions are important in the script?
- How would you play Scout's part from your reading of the script?
- What changes would you make to the way you might play Scout after reading the extract from the novel?
- From your readings of the novel and the script, how would you play Jem?
- How should the attacker be played?

 b) **Rehearse a performance** of the scene using the ideas you have explored in your discussion. One of you will need to take control of the sound effects vital to the scene.

Remember to:
- **vary your tone** to match the stage directions of the script
- use **sound effects** carefully to create tension.

④ Unit 8 Assignment: Self-help

Assessment Focuses

▶ **AF2** Produce texts which are appropriate to task, reader and purpose

▶ **AF3** Vary sentences for clarity, purpose and effect

You: are a writer.

Your task: to write a self-help leaflet on fears and how to overcome them, aimed at young people. The leaflet is mainly an information text but it also includes advice.

• •

Stage 1

Plan your leaflet using the information provided below.

Paragraph 1
Refer back to pages 171–172 and find the information about what fears are in the webpage text. Look particularly at the subheading 'The difference between a fear and a phobia'. Focus on gathering information on fears, not phobias. Also use your answer to question 10 on page 176 to help you define the idea of 'rational fear'. Draw on this information to write your introduction.

Paragraph 2
Study the notes opposite. Include a linking paragraph giving information on stressful situations. Don't include every example – select the best information.

> **We are under stress in many situations. For example:**
> ● examinations
> ● performing on stage
> ● job interviews
> ● driving tests
> ● visiting the dentist
> ● going out on a first date.

Paragraph 3

Include a paragraph on how to overcome fears. This time use all the information from the notes below. Create a 'Good Advice' text box summarising four useful tips for overcoming fears.

> **We can help overcome fear:**
> ● through relaxation exercises – for example, deep breathing, meditation, slow exercise.
> ● through confidence building – for example, setting achievable targets
> ● by taking up a challenge – for example, in sport
> ● by talking through problems.

Stage 2

Use ICT to **plan the layout** of your leaflet. Think about:
● headings and subheadings
● font sizes
● positioning of your advice text box
● pictures or symbols from a suitable program.

Stage 3

Write and **set out your leaflet using ICT**. Consider these points:
● use the present tense for presenting things as they are
● use an informal, chatty tone
● explain any unfamiliar or technical terms you include
● use imperative verbs in your advice box (for example, 'Make sure…', 'Try to…')

Remember: use a range of ICT tools and save your work.

187

Unit 9 Growing pains

① The phone call

Aims

▶ Read an extract from *The Lost Boys Appreciation Society*

▶ Learn about characters who also are narrators (Wr5)

▶ Learn about contrasts of mood

▶ Learn about figures of speech

▶ Write an account from another character's perspective

The following text is an extract from *The Lost Boys Appreciation Society* by Alan Gibbons. Gary is flicking cold baked beans at his older brother John and being generally irritating, while their father is in the loft looking for something for their mother, who is out. Then the phone rings…

Quite how long it had been ringing before I heard it I'm not sure. The house was bedlam that afternoon, all Gary's fault of course. He had just been flicking cold baked beans at me and slipped out of reach as I took a swipe at him.

5 Dr-ing.

I jerked to attention. I seemed to understand right away that the call was urgent. I went to get up from the table but Gary started calling me names so I took another swipe at him.

Dr-ing.

10 Somehow the tone seemed more insistent, almost shrill.

'Give over,' I said. 'Can't you hear the phone ringing?'

Gary could hear all right but he didn't care. That's the way it is with Gary, he never knows when to stop, he thinks he's Jack the lad, a real funny guy. The truth is he's training to be the world's

15 greatest pillock. In fact, it's the only thing he puts any effort into,

his pillockness. He flicked another cold congealed lump of beany gunge in my direction, spattering my new Ellesse top. It had been flawlessly cream and cool until Gary got to work on it. That did it. I finally flipped and sprang at him. I was coming round the corner of the table when I met resistance. My legs suddenly stiffened and stopped working. Before I could do a thing about it I stumbled, pitched forward and fell flat on my face. Gary had tied my shoelaces together without me noticing! How could he do that? I didn't feel a thing.

'How old *are* you?' I yelled as I rolled over onto my back. 'That's a stupid kid's trick.'

Dr-ing.'

The prolonged ringing was beginning to worry me. Whoever was on the other end wasn't giving up. They were determined to get an answer. Desperate – and in my mind desperation equals importance.

'Gary, will you get that!'

He just laughed. The spectacle of me rolling round like an upturned beetle was clearly far more entertaining than something as mundane as answering the phone. I was still trying to unknot my laces when Dad came stamping downstairs. I heard him pick up the handset.

'Didn't either of you hear it?' he grumbled. 'I was up in the loft trying to find your mum's sewing machine before she gets home. You'd think you could do one little thing for me.'

'I heard it,' I snapped, 'but El Divvo here tied my shoelaces together.'

Dad was still barking at us when someone spoke at the other end.

'You behave yourself, Gary,' said Dad. 'No argument.'

Gary tried to come back with a smart riposte. He has an answer for everything, our Gary. But Dad wasn't in the mood.

'Just shut it!' he yelled.

The caller must have objected at that point because Dad immediately said, 'No, not you,'

There was a moment's hesitation, then a sound like something bursting, imploding, but far away, as though somebody had pulled

189

the plug on the day. I finally undid my laces and walked to the door. It was for all the world as if the air had been completely sucked out of the hallway. Something was wrong. The anger-flash had drained out of Dad's face, replaced by a blank pallor.

Like disbelief –

Like horror – 'Say – that – again.'

His voice trailed away into the half-light, the final word disintegrating into the dusk. Gary had joined me in the doorway. He too had heard the implosion, a sound beyond hearing, almost, a resonance that shuddered through the house, pulling down certainties. I was looking at Dad, trying to make eye contact, but he continued to stare ahead.

'Dad?'

He held up his hand. His Adam's apple was working strangely in his throat as if he were choking noiselessly. I remembered what he had been doing in the loft – looking for Mum's sewing machine.

Hers.

My mum's.

The link was made in my mind. Suddenly, as if it had been whispered into my ear by some evil spirit. I knew exactly what the call was about. I questioned Dad with my eyes but still he wouldn't return the look. I was making a silent plea, begging it not to be bad news, begging it not to be her. Then I watched Dad's hand go to his face and cover his mouth. Time stood still as his eyes shut tight, squeezing away the threatening tears. He refused to let them come. Even then, even at that moment when our lives broke apart, he continued to play the game. Big boys don't cry.

bedlam uproar; originally Bedlam was the name of an asylum
riposte clever reply

Key Reading

Narrative texts

This text is a story or **narrative**. The **purpose** of a narrative is to entertain us.

The main features of this text are:

● It has a structure that includes an **introduction**, a problem or **complication**, a **crisis** and a **resolution** when things are sorted out. The opening may introduce a setting, a character or an event.

● It has **expressive** and **descriptive** language (powerful verbs, nouns, adjectives and figurative language) to maintain the interest of the reader. The language can be comic: 'he's training to be the world's greatest pillock…' or serious: 'I was making a silent plea, begging it not to be bad news…'

● It has a **narrator** who tells the story in the first person (I) or the third person (he/she/it), for example: '*I* took a swipe at him.' (first person).

● It has clearly drawn **characters**. In this case the **narrator** is the main character, but a minor character can also be a narrator.

1 How would you describe the two brothers at the **beginning** of the extract? How do they **change** later?

2 Why does John think the phone must be answered? Which **word** signals this?

3 Which **verb** at the start of paragraph 3 also indicates that something odd is about to happen?

4 What **tense** is the story mainly told in?

. . . .

Purpose

Some writers have a group of people in mind (their audience) before they begin writing.

5 Who might be the **target audience** for this book? Choose one option and say why:

- young children
- people interested in family narratives
- boys

- adults
- teenagers
- girls.

. . . .

Reading for meaning

John is both the main character and the narrator, so the story is told from his point of view. It is a first-person narration. For example:

> 'Quite how long it had been began ringing I'm not sure.'

narrative story
narrator who is telling the story
narration how the story is told

first-person narration

In a first-person narration the character is often looking back and recounting the events. We gain a clear picture of his thoughts and feelings, relating to him or her, or empathising with him or her.

Wr5

6 Think about the main event in the extract. Why does the story **suit a first-person narration**?

7 a) Using evidence from the extract, make some quick notes on **John's character**. Focus on:

- his attitude to Gary and his father

- his response to the phone ringing and what this tells you about him.

b) Also make notes on his **role as the narrator**. For example, what do the lines below tell you about his attitude to Gary? You could briefly select some key words that give you clues.

'That's the way it is with Gary, he never knows when to stop, he thinks he's Jack the lad, a real funny guy.'

useful key words

c) Use your notes to **write a short character sketch** of John.

• •

Focus on: Contrasts

You may remember that the mood or tone of a piece of writing is the kind of feeling created. For example, in the extract on pages 188–190, the tension gradually builds up so that the mood of anxiety develops into one of fear.

In this extract, however, there is a sudden change of mood when the phone is answered. So the language changes; it becomes more figurative and less everyday. We quickly realise that something shocking has happened.

Read the example below. Then read the notes carefully.

> There was a moment's hesitation, then a sound like something bursting, imploding, but far away, as though somebody had pulled the plug on the day.

vivid images create a 'concrete' picture in the reader's mind

the images suggest a picture of something major (such as a world or planet) coming to an end

By creating 'concrete' pictures, the writer is able to signal the enormity of what has happened.

8 a) In pairs, **identify three vivid images** in this short extract from the text.

> His voice trailed away into the half-light, the final word disintegrating into the dusk. Gary had joined me in the doorway. He too had heard the implosion, a sound beyond hearing, almost, a resonance that shuddered through the house, pulling down certainties.

b) Discuss what each image reminds you of. Note down any concrete pictures that come to mind.

Key Writing

9 a) In pairs, discuss **what Gary is like** from the information you have in the extract. You should both **make notes**.

Look back at the work you did on John in question 7a), but this time focus on Gary. What is his:

- attitude to John
- response to the phone ringing
- response to his father
- general view of the world
- change in attitude when the phone is answered?

b) Compare your notes and make any changes to your own as a result of your discussion. Decide together roughly **how old** Gary is.

c) Now use your notes to **write the events from Gary's point of view**. His point of view is likely to differ from John's, particularly over events in the first part of the extract.

Remember to:

- begin when the phone starts ringing and include its ringing in your account
- use a first-person narration and the past tense
- change the language you use. For example, the reader should feel the change from the everyday language of the boys fooling around, to the more figurative language of being in a state of shock.

② The boy next door?

Aims

▶ Read a discursive text

▶ Identify the issue and the arguments in the text

▶ Learn about the active and passive tenses (S3)

▶ Carry out group discussion and come to an agreement (S&L9)

The following article is from a website. Are you surprised at the comments?

Boys, it seems, are at the top of the agenda again

I switched on the television the other day to see some expert being interviewed on the crisis of boys' underachievement in school, compared to girls' achievement.

Yes that old chestnut.

5 So I was about to switch off when the speaker suddenly became animated. 'Boys', he announced… 'well…no wonder they underachieve.' It's all to do with their hormones.'

Youths of a certain age it seems have a natural tendency towards aggression, lawlessness, antisocial behaviour, non-communication, dislike
10 of authority (that's anyone from the bus driver to the high-court judge) and are emotionally inept. And it's all down to testosterone overload.

Can this be true?

Only when they reach adulthood do they strive for their place in society, he went on. Then apparently antisocial behaviour is useful for
15 fighting your way to the top.

I thought of the boy next door – that mild-mannered, good-natured, articulate teenage boy. Was he really a wolf in sheep's clothing?

No. Not according to a second speaker.

20 Boys are perfectly capable of managing their behaviour. It all depends on the context.

You mean they're just like the rest of us?

But there was more. Boys, it seems, don't really like education. It's boring. It has low status. And if you want to be one of the boys…

25 Then up popped a clip of half a dozen young men lounging against a wall. They must have been about fourteen or fifteen years old and were being questioned by a roving reporter. How did they see themselves in relation to girls? This was the third group of boys who'd been
30 interviewed; they came from all sorts of backgrounds and they all said the same.

Boys are definitely different from girls. Boys like football. Girls like talk. Boys like a laugh. Girls like talk. Boys like a rumble. Girls like… You get the picture.

35 They didn't think much of talk. What was it for? Winding people up?

But there were some good things about girls, they said. They were sympathetic. They were sensible. They thought it was important to work and do well in exams. And crucially, they were different from boys.

The reporter was confused. 'So boys don't care about exams?' He
40 was met with blank faces. 'So boys do care about exams?'

'Yeah – course.' All heads nodded.

On a more serious note it seems boys, like girls, do want to achieve academically, but they don't want to be seen as boffins. Some of this has been backed up by research. Experts suggest that boys' views on
45 gender difference are not fixed but 'dependent on the situation boys find themselves in.'

So I suppose if achieving academically really meant you were man of the match…

But can it be as simple as that?
50 I decided to ask someone else.

What did my football-crazy, inarticulate, moody, morose, fourteen-year-old daughter think about all this?

'Boys? Boys? I mean 'hullo'. They're like so…' She was lost for words.
55 They're like…so… "duh!"'

I wonder what the boy next door would say?

---

animated lively

hormones substances in the body that can affect mood and behaviour

emotionally inept unable to express feelings easily

testosterone male hormone; used casually to refer to drive and aggression

gender difference differences between the sexes

inarticulate unable to express oneself clearly

Key Reading

Discursive texts

This is a **discursive** text. The **purpose** of discursive writing is to present an argument from different points of view.

This main features of this text are:

- It has a **form** that consists of an **opening statement**, **a series of points** on both sides of the issue and evidence supporting these points. For example, 'Some of this has been backed up by research'.

- It has **sentence signposts** or **key words** to signal which side of the issue you are writing about. Sometimes sentences are in the form of a question. For example, 'Was he really a wolf in sheep's clothing? No. Not according to a second speaker.'

- It uses the **present tense**, but the **past tense** is also used.

- It uses some formal **language**, for example, '…it seems boys, like girls, do want to achieve academically'. **Informal language** is also used frequently to engage the reader, for example, 'Yes, that old chestnut.'

1 What does the **opening sentence** mean?

2 a) What is the **main issue** in the text?

   b) Which **paragraph** tells you what the issue is? Write down the **sentence signpost**.

3 Do you think the text is mainly written in **formal or informal language**?

4 a) Are the following written in the **present or past tense**?

- 'I switched on the television the other day...'
- 'Youths of a certain age, it seems,...
- '...they aspire to be top dog.'

b) Why are **both tenses** used?

. . . .

Purpose

5 a) What is the main purpose of **discursive texts**?

b) What is the main purpose of **this text**?

6 Which two groups of people do you think would be **most interested** in the issue? Choose from the list below and say why.

- pupils
- boys
- girls
- teachers
- parents.

. . . .

Reading for meaning

The **main issue** is not the same as the two arguments in the text. Look back at the answers you gave to question 2. You should have noted that the main issue focuses on 'boys' underachievement in school'.

The **arguments** present reasons for this underachievement. In other words they ask 'why?' You can find the first argument by asking 'why' and looking for sentence signposts or key words. For example:

Question	Argument 1	Where
Why do boys underachieve in school?	'It's all to do with their hormones.'	Paragraph 5

7 a) Make **your own copy** of the table.

b) In pairs, discuss what Argument 1 means and why it might lead boys to underachieve at school. For example: 'hormones' are related to physical changes in adolescence. *This suggests that boys can't help these changes.*

Argument 1 is backed up by **evidence** in paragraph 4. Read this and add another column to your table like this:

Evidence
'This makes boys...' (paragraph 4)

Then discuss how the evidence relates to boys' underachievement.

8 In the same way, find Argument 2 and the evidence given to back it up and add this information to your table. (Remember: Argument 2 is opposed to Argument 1.)

Argument 2 is also more complex, so look carefully for key words or signposts that tell you *why boys underachieve.* For example, discuss what the boys say to the reporter in paragraph 15. Does this support Argument 2 or not?

• •

Focus on: Using the passive form

Both the active and passive forms are used in the text. The active 'voice' speaks directly to the reader. The passive 'voice' is more formal and distant. For example:

> **Active form:**
>
> I switched on the television.

'I' is the subject of the sentence   verb   'television' is the object of the action

Passive form:

The television was switched on by me.

'television' is the subject

verb

'I' becomes the passive agent of the sentence – 'by me'

S3

9 **a)** The following sentence is in the active form. Change it into the **passive**.

'Research has backed some of this up.'

b) Now look in paragraph 14 to **find the sentence** you have rewritten.

Sometimes the agent (or 'by' phrase) is dropped because it would be overstating the point. For example, find this sentence in paragraph 13:

'The reporter was confused.'

This really means:

'The reporter was confused (by the boys).'

The agent is dropped

10 Change the following into the **passive**. Decide whether or not to use the agent.

- The reporter questioned them.
- They all shared the same opinion.
- Boys like football.

Key Speaking and Listening

 11 a) Work in a group to **discuss both sides** of this issue.

S&L9

> Why do boys underachieve in school?

- Use the notes you made earlier about Arguments 1 and 2 in the text to start your discussion.
- Develop your ideas by building on each other's points.
- Back up what you say by pointing to evidence and examples.
- Try to agree on your view as a group. (For example, you could agree on one point of view, neither point of view or think that both views have merit.)

All members of the group should **make notes** on the main points from your discussion. You will need these to complete the assignment on page 209.

b) Choose one person to **report your findings** to another group. Ask them for feedback and add any new points to your notes.

Chinese Cinderella

Aims

▷ Read from an autobiography

▷ Study the use of powerful language

▷ Study the preface to the autobiography

▷ Write a recount from a particular perspective (R6)

The following text is an extract from *Chinese Cinderella* by Adeline Yen Mah. Adeline lives with her father, stepmother and extended family. One evening her father decides to test the obedience of the family dog, Jackie, using Adeline's pet duckling, PLT (Precious Little Treasure).

Father released PLT and placed her in the centre of the lawn. My little pet appeared bewildered by all the commotion. She stood quite still for a few moments, trying to get her bearings: a small, yellow, defenceless creature beset with perils, surrounded by humans wanting to test their dog in a gamble with her life. I sat stiffly with downcast eyes. For a

5 moment, I was unable to focus properly. 'Don't move, PLT! Please don't move!' I prayed silently. 'As long as you keep still, you have a chance!'

Jackie was ordered to 'sit' about two metres away. He sat on his hind legs with his large tongue hanging out, panting away. His fierce

10 eyes were riveted on his prey. Father kept two fingers on his collar while the German Shepherd fidgeted and strained restlessly.

The tension seemed palpable while I hoped against hope that fate could be side-stepped in some way. Then PLT cocked her head in that achingly familiar way of hers and spotted me. Chirping happily, she

15 waddled unsteadily towards me. Tempted beyond endurance, Jackie sprang forward. In one powerful leap, he broke away from Father's restraint and pounced on PLT, who looked up at me pleadingly, as if I was supposed to have an answer to all her terror. Father dashed over, enraged by Jackie's defiance. Immediately, Jackie released the bird

20 from his jaws, but with a pang I saw PLT's left leg dangling lifelessly and her tiny, webbed foot twisted at a grotesque angle. Blood spurted briskly from an open wound.

I was overwhelmed with horror. My whole world turned desolate. I ran over without a word, cradled PLT tenderly in my arms and carried her upstairs. Placing her on my bed, I wrapped my mortally wounded pet in my best school scarf and lay down next to her. It was a night of grief I have never forgotten.

I lay there with my eyes closed pretending to be asleep but was actually hopelessly awake. Surely everything would remain the same as long as I kept my eyes shut and did not look at PLT. Perhaps, when I finally opened them again after wishing very hard all night, PLT's leg would miraculously be healed.

Though it was the height of summer and Aunt Baba had lowered the mosquito net over my bed, I was deathly cold; thinking over and over, 'When tomorrow comes, will PLT be all right?'

In spite of everything, I must have dozed off because at the break of dawn I woke up with a jerk. Beside me, PLT was now completely still. The horrors of the previous evening flooded back and everything was as bad as before. Worse, because PLT was now irrevocably dead. Gone forever.

Almost immediately, I heard Father calling Jackie in the garden. He was preparing to take his dog for their customary Sunday morning walk. At the sound of Jackie's bark, Aunt Baba suddenly sat up in her bed. 'Quick! Take this opportunity while Jackie's away! Run down and bury your pet in the garden. Get the big spade from the tool shed at the back and dig a proper hole.' She handed me an old sewing box, placed PLT's little body inside and closed the lid.

I dashed out of my room and almost collided with Big Brother, who had just come out of the bathroom into the hall.

'Where are *you* going?' he asked, full of curiosity. 'And what's that you're carrying?'

'I'm going to the garden to bury PLT.'

'Bury her! Why don't you give her to Cook and ask him to stew her for breakfast instead? Stewed duck in the evening and stewed duck in the morning! I love the taste of duck, don't you?' He saw the look on my face and knew he had gone too far. 'Look, that was a joke. I didn't really mean it. I'm sorry about last night too. I didn't know which duckling to pick when Father gave me that order. I only took yours because you're the one least likely to give me trouble afterwards. It wasn't anything against you personally, understand?'

'She was my best friend in the whole world...' I began, tears welling up in spite of myself. 'And now I've lost her forever.'

palpable a feeling that is so strong
    it can almost be touched

mortally fatally, causing death

Key Reading

Autobiography

The text is both an **autobiography** and a **recount**. Its **purpose** is to tell the reader about a series of events – in this case Adeline Yen Mah's early memories.

The main features of this text are:

● It is told in the **first person, 'I'**, and the **past tense**, for example, 'I sat stiffly with downcast eyes.'

● It uses **time connectives**, for example, 'For a moment…'

● It is usually told in **chronological order**, for example, 'at the break of dawn, I woke up with a jerk'.

● It includes **specific facts** from the writer's past, for example, the names of her family – Big Brother and Aunt Baba.

● It includes **personal feelings**, for example, 'I was overwhelmed with horror'.

1 Think of **three powerful words** that would describe most readers' reaction to the episode.

2 Find an **example** in the text that shows:

a) the awful cruelty of the events

b) a character who is kind to Adeline.

3 Why do you think Adeline **didn't protest** when her father placed PLT on the lawn?

4 **Complete a table** like the one below for all five of the features of autobiography texts. Use the text-type box for information and give examples from the extract where you can. The first has been done for you.

Features of autobiography	Example
Written in the past tense	'She *stood* quite still'

Purpose

5 **Why** do you think Adeline wrote about her life?

Reading for meaning

There are several powerful descriptions in the extract. For example, PLT is described as:

a… defenceless creature beset with perils…

powerful adjective   powerful verb

6 **a)** Identify the **powerful adjectives and verbs** in the following short extract:

> I ran over without a word, cradled PLT tenderly in my arms and carried her upstairs. Placing her on the bed, I wrapped my mortally wounded pet in my best school scarf and lay down next to her.

b) Write them down under the headings 'Verbs' and 'Adjectives'.

7 **a)** Sometimes a powerful description or statement about one thing can tell us about another. Study this description of PLT again:

Quotation	Notes
'a… defenceless creature beset with perils'	This describes PLT, but it could also describe Adeline.

b) In pairs, read the following statement. **Scan the text** to find it.

> He was preparing to take his dog for their customary Sunday morning walk.

c) What can you tell about Adeline's father from this statement? Discuss your ideas together.

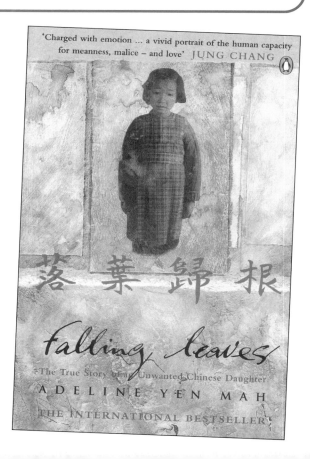

'Charged with emotion … a vivid portrait of the human capacity for meanness, malice – and love' JUNG CHANG

落 葉 歸 根

falling leaves

The True Story of an Unwanted Chinese Daughter

ADELINE YEN MAH

THE INTERNATIONAL BESTSELLER

. . . .

Focus on: Dedications

Adeline dedicates her book to 'all unwanted children'.
She also writes:

> Chinese Cinderella is my autobiography. It was difficult and painful to write but I felt compelled to do so. Though mine is but a simple, personal tale of my childhood, please do not underestimate the power of such stories. In one way or another every one of us has been shaped and moulded by the stories we have read and absorbed in the past. All stories, including fairy-tales, present elemental truths which can sometimes permeate your inner life and become part of you.

8 When Adeline says that we should not underestimate the 'power' of stories from childhood, she means they can affect us deeply. In pairs, discuss whether you think such stories **have to be true** or not. Why?

A **preface** is a statement from the writer which comes before the main text. The comment above comes from the preface to Adeline Yen Mah's book. It is written in a different style from the extract.

R6 **9** Copy down the table below. First, write the **answers** in column 1. Then find **examples** in the preface and write them down in column 2.

Features of the preface	Example
Why was it written? (Its purpose) Answer:	
What tense is it mainly written in? Answer:	
Is it written in the first or third person? Answer:	

Key Writing

10 a) Adeline buries PLT in the garden with the help of Third Brother, who is sometimes kind to her. This is partly because of his own position in the family.

Imagine you are Adeline and **write a recount of the burial**. Use the first person ('I') and the past tense. Include the following details:

- PLT is buried in a small box under the magnolia tree.
- The tree is in bloom.
- Food is left for PLT: some grains of rice, a few worms, some water in a dish.
- A bunch of flowers is left in a milk bottle by the grave.

Try to capture Adeline's sorrow by commenting on one of these features of the scene. For example, in the autobiography we are told:

> I was never able to smell the fragrance of magnolia blossoms again without the same aching sense of loss.

b) Now **write a paragraph of preface** to this extract. Focus on why you as Adeline have included it. Remember to write in the first person ('I') and in the present tense.

④ Unit 9 Assignment: The journalist

Assessment Focus

▶ AF4 Construct paragraphs and use cohesion within and between paragraphs

---

You: are a journalist.

Your task: to write a discursive article for a school magazine discussing the issue of boys' underachievement.

•••••••••••••••••••••••••••••••••

Stage 1

Remember: when you write a discursive account you consider the issue through a number of arguments.

Create a plan for the main part of your article by copying down the headings below. Then quickly refer to your notes from question 11 on page 201 and write down the issue and arguments. Make sure you understand the two main arguments.

The issue:

Argument 1:

Argument 2:

Stage 2

Again using your notes, highlight or underline the **main points** and the **evidence** from each argument.

For example, Argument 1 might begin:

'Changes boys undergo in adolescence make them...'

What other points and evidence would you highlight?

Repeat this process for Argument 2. Remember that it is opposed to Argument 1.

Complete your plan by adding notes for:

- an opening statement that introduces the issue
- a conclusion in which you weigh up the arguments.

Stage 3

Write your account, following the structure of your plan. Try to include these features:

- a brief opening statement about the issue
- evidence to support Arguments 1 and 2
- a range of connectives (for example, to explain cause and effect: *because, so, consequently, therefore*; to compare and contrast: *on the one hand, on the other hand, in the same way, alternatively, whereas*)
- formal language, including the passive if appropriate
- a short conclusion about the issue and arguments put forward.

Aims

▶ Find out more about testing in English and how to do your best
▶ Practise some skills related to test and assessment work

Why are students assessed?

It is important for you, your teachers, and your parents to know what you can do well, and what you need more help with. For example, questions can test how well you have read and understood a text.

Look at the extract below. It comes from the mock Reading Paper your teacher will give you to practise for the Key Stage 3 Test. The text is about Microsoft's plans to develop the human body as a communication device.

> Call it the ultimate wireless network. From the ends of your fingers to the tips of your toes, the human body is a moving, throbbing collection of tubes and tunnels, filled with salty water and all capable of transmitting the lifeblood of the 21st century: information.

Here are two questions you might be asked about the extract above:

> 1) What is a 'moving, throbbing collection of tubes and tunnels'?
>
> 2) What words or phrases does the writer use to paint a vivid picture of the human body?

1 **a)** Which of the two questions on page 212 do you think is
more difficult? Think about:
- which one asks you for a **single answer**
- which one asks you to make a judgement by asking you to
  look at **several things**.

b) Try to **answer the questions**.

The questions are designed to test different levels of
understanding in reading skills. That is the point of the test.

. . . .

Why don't teachers just look at class and homework?

It is good practice to get used to these tests, since you will have to
do tests at GCSE and beyond. Your teacher can then also be sure
that you and the rest of the class have completed the assessment
under the same conditions.

. . . .

What is the real Key Stage 3 English Test like?

There are **three** papers (or parts of the test).

The Reading Paper

- This paper consists of **three** different texts/extracts (for
  example, these could be an extract from a story, a report, and
  an advertisement or leaflet).
- It also has questions on each text.
- It is worth **32 marks**.
- You have **1 hour 15 minutes** to read the extracts and answer
  the questions.

The Writing Paper

There are **two** writing tasks.

Section A contains the longer writing task. This asks you to write a well-developed response on a set topic. There is also a plan to help you.

● It is worth **30 marks**.

● You have **45 minutes** to complete the task (this includes 15 minutes planning time).

Section B contains the shorter writing task. The focus here is on writing a precise, focused, shorter piece of writing in response to a set topic. There is no planning frame to support you.

● It is worth **20 marks**, including 4 for spelling.

● You have **30 minutes** to complete the task.

The Shakespeare Paper

This includes **two** extracts from the set scenes from the play you are studying.

● It includes one task that tests your knowledge and understanding of the play.

● It is worth **18 marks**.

● It is based on the two scenes you have studied in detail.

● You have **45 minutes** to complete the paper.

Total marks for the Test:

Reading:	Reading Paper	32
	Shakespeare	18
Writing:	Longer writing task	30
	Shorter writing task	20
TOTAL marks:		100

Advice on the Reading Test

You will be assessed on **five** different areas.

1. **Your ability to *understand, describe, select or retrieve information from texts***

    This means looking at the text you have been given, then finding information you have been asked for. Sometimes you will be asked to explain this information.

2. **Your ability to *deduce, infer or interpret information***

    This means explaining something from the text that might not be so obvious, for example, where a writer suggests something, but doesn't say it directly.

3. **Your ability to *comment on the overall structure of the text***

    This means explaining how the text is organised, for example, saying how the beginning and end of the text are linked.

4. **Your ability to *explain and comment on the writer's use of language***

    This means explaining how and why the writer chose individual words and phrases.

5. **Your ability to *identify and comment on the writer's purpose and viewpoint, and the overall effect of the text***

    This means explaining what the writer was trying to do, or the point he or she wanted to make, and how effective it was.

Practising Reading Test skills

Skill 1: Reading the question

People always say 'read the question carefully!', but what does that mean? Each question tests a different skill, as you have seen.

Imagine you have just read a leaflet arguing against animal cruelty. Here is a possible question from the test:

> How many cases of animal cruelty are there each year, according to the leaflet? (1 mark)

Let's see what you need to do. First of all, highlight the key words as follows:

Tells us we are looking for a number (of cases)

Tells us that we should look for this, not other types of case

> **How many cases** of **animal cruelty** are there **each year,** according to the leaflet? (1 mark)

Means we should ignore other information about longer periods of time

Pay attention to the marks. Only **one** is available here, so you are likely to be looking for **one** answer or point

2 Highlight the **key words** in this question:

> Which two types of animal are most likely to be used in animal testing? (2 marks)

Skill 2: Short and long answers

You have already seen how the number of marks can provide guidance when you are answering a reading question, but how else can marks help?

The Reading Test has 32 marks. You have about one hour to read the questions, search for and write your answers (plus fifteen minutes overall reading time).

This means you have about **two minutes per mark**.

So if a question is worth four marks, you should spend between eight and ten minutes on it (you can speed up on the easier, one mark questions). Of course, you cannot stick to this completely. You will find some questions easier than others, but it will help you stick to the overall time limit.

3 Look back at the text on pages 147–148. Write down two things from the first paragraph that tell us Sipho's family is quite poor.

(2 marks)

Remember:
● check the **key words** in the question
● check the **number of marks**
● **read** the text quickly
● try to **answer** the question as **quickly** as you can.

A longer question might be:

How does the writer convey the impression that Sipho's family live in a poor and dangerous neighbourhood?   (5 marks)

For a question like this one you would be expected to write a longer answer and probably mention about five different ways or examples, as there are five marks.

4 Try to answer this question in approximately **ten minutes**.

Skill 3: Using evidence

Sometimes in the test you are given questions which ask you to think and give your view, and support it with evidence from the text. You may know the answer but not know how to put it into words or forget to support what you say (with evidence) and just write down what you think.

Look at this sample question, which is also based on the text on pages 147–148:

> Explain how the writer's use of language shows Sipho's fear as he tries to leave. Support your answer with at least two examples.
>
> (2 marks)

An incomplete answer to this question might be:

The writer shows how nervous and frightened Sipho is by the way he acts and moves, and how he is frightened about his stepfather and mother. He uses really good descriptions of how Sipho feels.

A more precise answer would be:

The writer describes how Sipho was 'tiptoeing' around his house, and how he 'held his breath' as he tried to leave. The writer also uses a simile to describe how Sipho's heart had been feeling – as 'tight as a fist'.

 5 Discuss with a partner **what is better** about the second response.

Tip

If you are asked for examples or quotations from the passage, make sure you include them. Look at page 152 for advice on how to use quotations – it does take skill to put them into your sentences.

Skill 4: Reading between the lines

This skill is more difficult, because you have to use your judgement and look beneath the surface to explain something. It is about making inferences and interpreting what the writer says. Read the following text:

> The hotel had swirly, highly-coloured wallpaper and a musty sort of smell which some people would have considered old-fashioned, charming and quaint. The meals were 'traditional' – that's to say, extremely well-cooked, very British, and with enormous portions – especially of sprouts. Lovely, if you like that kind of thing.

The writer does not say **directly** that he doesn't like the hotel, but he **implies** it by:

● using the phrase 'some people' – implies that he is not one of the people who would like the smell and the wallpaper

● using quotation marks around 'traditional', as if to suggest, it is out-of-date and boring

● using phrases that could mean other things (euphemisms) such as 'extremely well-cooked' instead of 'burnt' or 'over-cooked'

● possibly being sarcastic: 'Lovely, if you like that sort of thing…'

6 Read the text below. Try to work out what the **writer's opinion** is and discuss your ideas with a partner.

> If you want a story with characters and feelings, then this isn't for you. But if you want a film with American accents you can't understand, men with tattoos and bulging muscles who eat their Cornflakes with their guns on the table, and more deaths than World War 2, then this film is definitely your cup of tea – or should I say, blood?

Advice on the Writing Test

The Writing Test contains **two** tasks – a longer, and a shorter one. The key skills assessed are outlined below:

The shorter writing task

1. **Sentence structure, punctuation and text organisation**

   This is the way your sentences are put together: the accuracy and effect of your use of punctuation; the way your writing fits together – how it makes sense and how it is organised, for example, whether your paragraphs help the reader to follow your line of thought.

2. **Composition and effect**

   This means the particular choices of words and phrases to fit the sort of text you are writing, for example, powerful description for narrative stories, clear vocabulary for advice texts, etc.; how well you interest the reader.

3. **Spelling**

   This means how well you spell words you are expected to know at your age, and tackle more difficult, complex or unfamiliar words. Spelling is not specifically assessed on the longer writing task.

The longer writing task

1. Sentence structure and punctuation

This means how clearly organised, fluent and effective your sentences are. Ask yourself:

● Have you used a variety of sentence structures (i.e. long, short, simple, complex) to fit the task?

● Have you used suitable connectives (joining words and phrases, such as 'however', 'despite' or 'in addition') to link sentences?

● Have you used a variety of verbs and verb forms to suit the writing task, for example, suitable tenses or 'modals such as 'should', 'may' or 'might'?

● Have you used punctuation (full-stops, commas, semicolons) to make meaning clear or for effect (for example, exclamation marks for disbelief: 'I was stunned!')?

2. Text structure and organisation

This means the overall structure and shape of the whole text, and how individual sections or ideas are linked together. Ask yourself:

● Have you written paragraphs with clear links to the subject you are writing about?

● Are your main ideas supported by evidence or other comments or details?

● Have you made the reader follow your line of thought? For example, have you led them towards the point you want to make?

● Have you considered a range of organisational devices, such as bullet points, subheadings or numbering?

3. Composition and effect

This means the appropriate style, form and language for the text you are writing, matched to the purpose of the text and, where relevant, the viewpoint of the writer. Ask yourself:

● Does your style match the form of the text (for example, if this is a formal business report, a chatty, personal style would not be suitable)? Have you kept this style throughout your piece?

● Have you shaped your writing to suit the reader? (For example, if you need to make an impact, have you used original ideas or language?)

● Have you used a suitable range of vocabulary – words, phrases and sentences – to fit the form (for example, in a report you might write, 'I have concluded from my analysis of the situation…')?

Use the bullet points above as a guide when completing the practice Writing Test.

Advice on the Shakespeare Paper

The Shakespeare Paper is a reading assessment, and therefore assesses the same basic areas as for the main Reading Paper. Below is a broad reminder of what is required.

The Play

You will have read and studied one play by Shakespeare. There are **two or three scenes** which you will prepare before the test, extracts from which appear in the Shakespeare Paper.

The Test

There is **one** task, which tests your knowledge and understanding of the play. It is worth **18 marks** and is based on the set scenes you have studied in detail. You have **45 minutes** to complete the test.

Preparation

The following exercises will help you prepare for the test.

- Describe the plot (the story) of the play to a friend in less than two minutes. Your friend should stop and correct you if you forget a key character or event.

- Write the name of a main character in the middle of an A4 sheet. Draw lines from that character and add at the end of each one another character and how they are connected to.

- Write the key themes from the play (such as ambition, love or disguise on a set of postcards.) Then write down a quotation from the play that matches the theme on one side, and one or two events that match the theme on the other side.

- Read one of your key scenes with a group of friends. Try to act out a basic version of the scene (in your own words) in five minutes.

- On your own, walk around your bedroom, kitchen or garden reading the lines from your key scenes aloud – this will help you get a sense of the sound and feeling of the language.

William Collins' dream of knowledge for all began with the publication of his first book in 1819. A self-educated mill worker, he not only enriched millions of lives, but also founded a flourishing publishing house. Today, staying true to this spirit, Collin packed with inspiration, innovation and practical expertise. They place you at the centre of a world of possibility and give you exactly what you need to explore it.

Collins. Do more.

Published by Collins
An imprint of HarperCollins*Publishers*
77–85 Fulham Palace Road
Hammersmith
London
W6 8JB

Browse the complete Collins catalogue at
www.collinseducation.com

© HarperCollins*Publishers* Limited 2005

10 9 8 7 6 5 4 3 2 1

ISBN 0 00 719438 2

Mike Gould, Mary Green, John Mannion and Kim Richardson assert their moral rights to be identified as the authors of this work

British Library Cataloguing in Publication Data
A Catalogue record for this publication is available from the British Library

Acknowledgements

The following permissions to reproduce material are gratefully acknowledged:

Text: Extract from 'The Mazarin Stone' taken from *The Case-Book of Sherlock Holmes* by Sir Arthur Conan Doyle, pp4–5; extract from *Master of the Rings: Inside the World of J.R.R. Tolkien* by Susan Ang (Wizard Books, 2002), pp11–12; review of 'Catch me if you can' from channel4.com, pp17–18; extract from *The Mother Tongue* by Bill Bryson (Penguin Books, 1991), pp26–27; 'Online words take wing' from *The Sunday Times*, pp33–34; extract from *Eats, Shoots & Leaves: The Zero Tolerance Approach to Punctuation* by Lynn Truss (Profile Books, 2003), pp40–41; extract from *The Complete Idiot's Guide to Elvis* by Frank Coffey (Alpha Books, 1997), pp48–49; inauguration speech by Nelson Mandela extracted from *In His Own Words*, edited by Kader Asmal and David Chidester (Little Brown and Company, 2003), pp54–55; 'How to write a letter to someone famous from justdosomething.net, pp61–62; 'On the eighth day' by Claire Calman © Claire Calman 2000 from *The Pop! Anthology (New Departures 2000)* edited by Michael Horovitz and Inge Elsa Laird, pp70–71; extract from 'Of Jeoffrey, His Cat' by Christopher Smart, p75; 'When we two parted' by Lord Byron, pp77–78; 'Anancy's Thoughts on Love' by John Agard from *Touchstones 5*, edited by Michael Benton and Peter Benton (Hodder and Stoughton, 1988), p79; 'Homeward Bound' and 'Neighbours' by Benjamin Zephaniah from *Propa Propaganda* (Bloodaxe Books, 2000) © Benjamin Zephaniah 1996, pp85–87; extract from *Stone Cold: The Play* by Joe Standerline, based on the novel by Robert Swindells (Nelson Thornes, 1999), pp96–97; Thames Reach Bondway poster and website reproduced with permission. Copy by Jeremy Swain, pp102–103; extract from *As I Walked Out One Midsummer Morning* by Laurie Lee (Penguin, 1971), pp108–109; 'Katie believes in God and marriage. Her mother doesn't' by Liz Lightfoot, from the *Daily Telegraph*, 11 March 2004, pp118–119; 'How to...go to a party' by Guy Browning from *The Guardian*, 4 October 2003, pp132–133; 'Letter to Daniel' by Fergal Keane, first broadcast on BBC Radio4, February 1996, pp140–141; extract from *No Turning Back* by Beverly Naidoo (Penguin, 2004), pp147–148; 'Tiger tracking in Rajasthan' from *Nature Journeys* by Dwight Holing (Weldon Owen Inc, 1996), pp154–155; extract from *The Woman in Black* by Susan Hill (Vintage, 1998), pp164–165; 'What is a phobia' from pe2000.com, pp171–172; extract from *To Kill a Mockingbird: Play* by Christopher Sergal, based on the novel by Harper Lee (Heinemann, 1995), pp178–180; extract from *To Kill a Mockingbird* by Harper Lee (Heinemann, 1960), p184; extract from *The Lost Boys' Appreciation Society* by Alan Gibbons (Orion Children's Books, 2004), pp188–190; extract from *Chinese Cinderella* by Adeline Yen Mah (Penguin, 1999), pp203–204.

Images: Alamy: pp66, 87, 143; Aquarius: pp18, 21; Tim Archbold, Graham Cameron Illustration: pp71, 73, 75; Ardea: 155, 157, 171, 176; Corbis: pp58, 86, 131, 146, 150, 151, 153, 168, 206; Bob Farley: Graham Cameron Illustration: pp7, 10, 24; Getty Images: pp16, 32, 36, 45, 49, 53, 55, 61, 67, 90, 101, 107, 113, 114, 119, 121, 125, 133, 137, 139, 159, 161, 174, 187, 189, 202, 211; Robert Harding: p109; Moviestore: pp12, 14, 179, 183; Penguin Books: 207; Nicola Taylor, NB Illustration: 78, 79, 95.

Whilst every effort has been made both to contact the copyright holders and to give exact credit lines, this has not proved possible in every case.

Printed and bound by Printing Express, Hong Kong